# Santa

## Coloring Book

## This Book Belongs to:

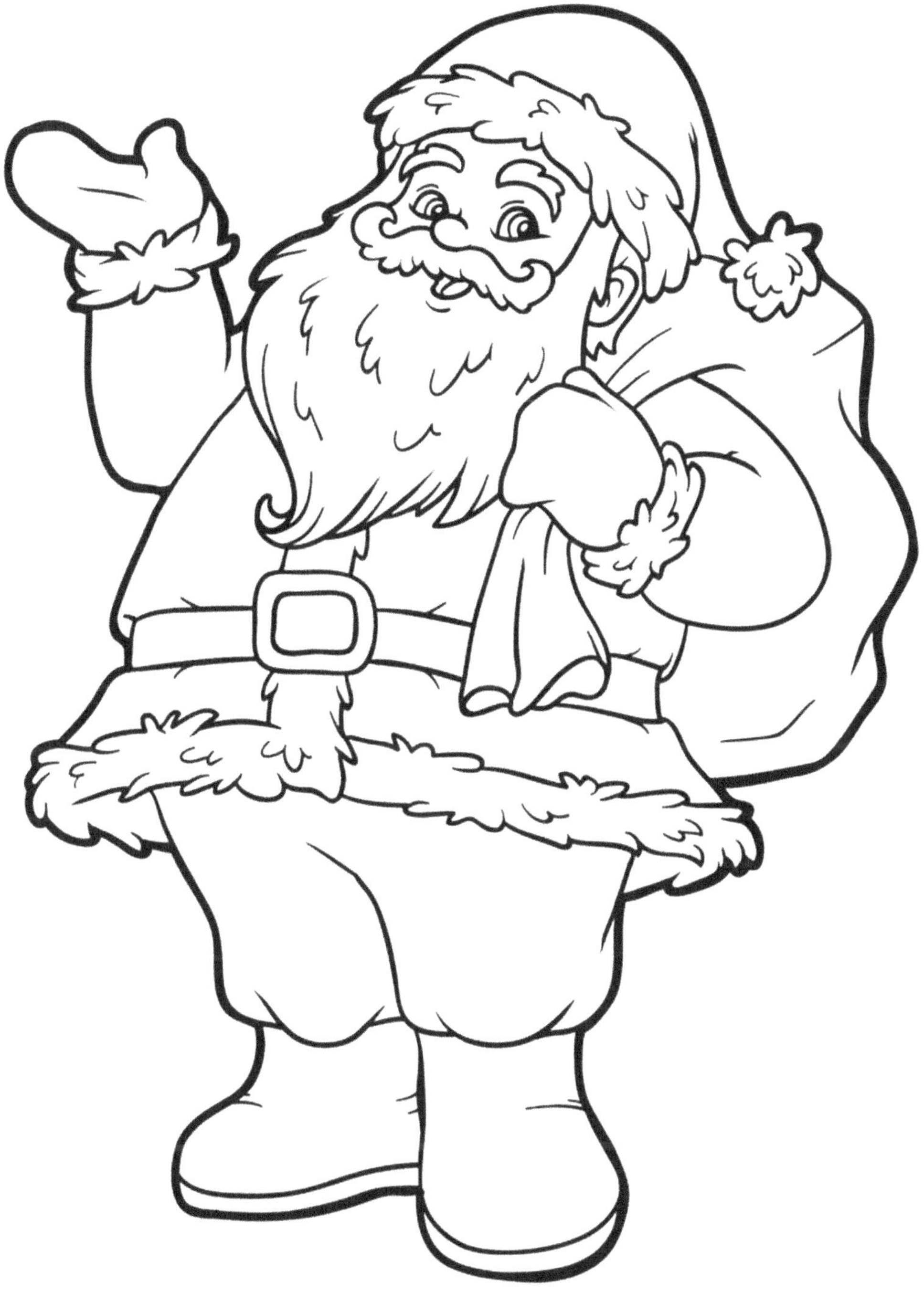

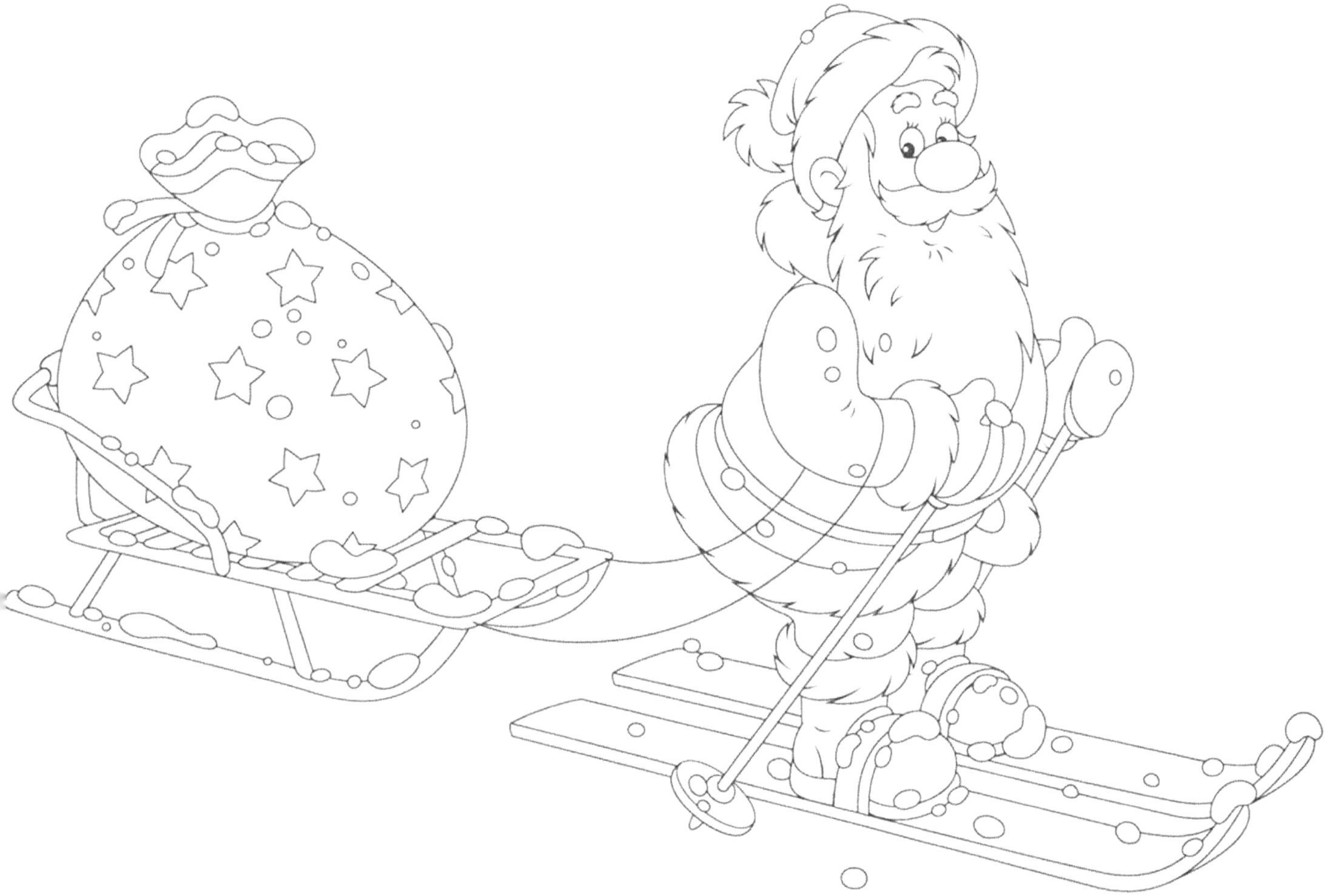

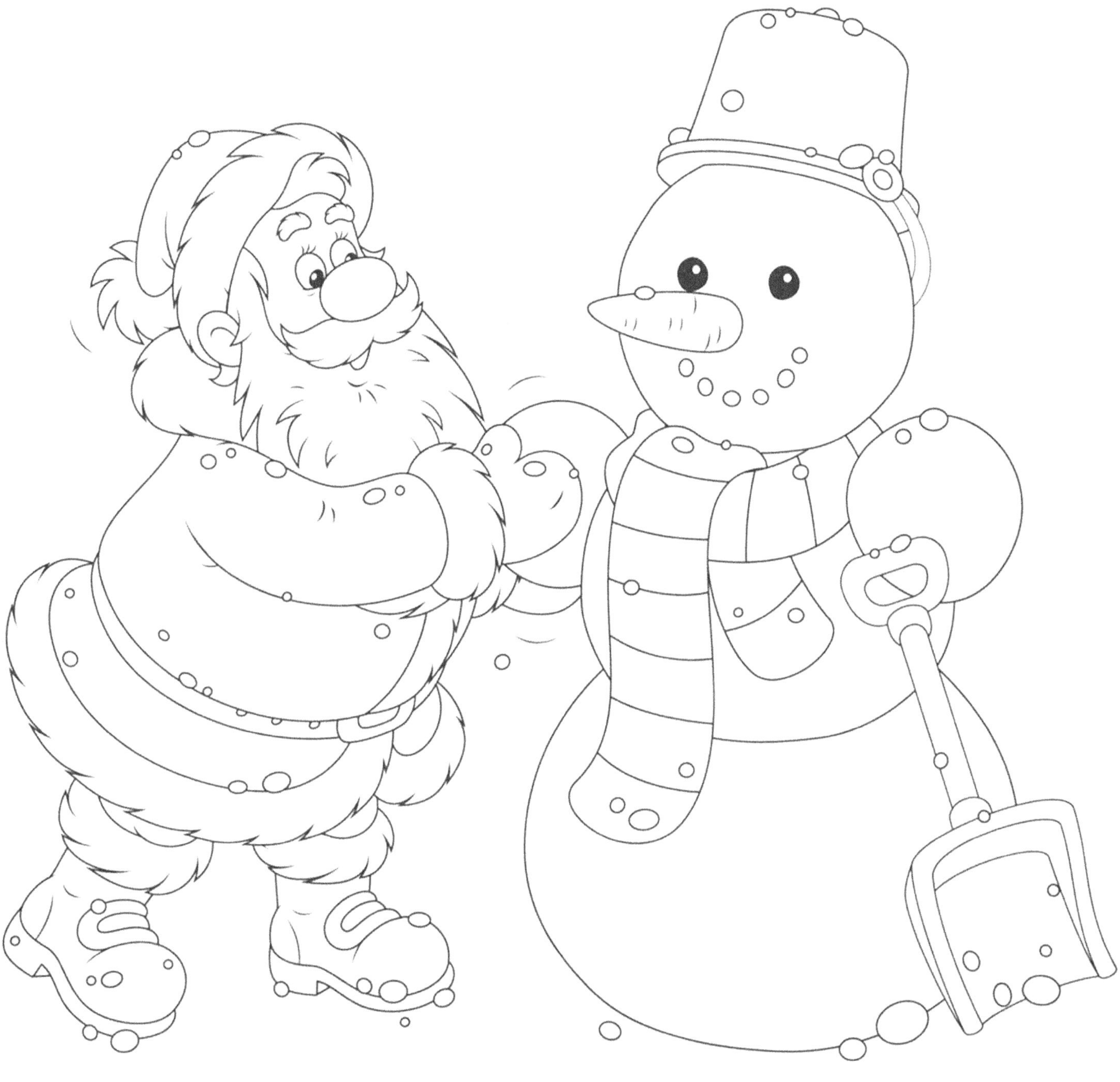

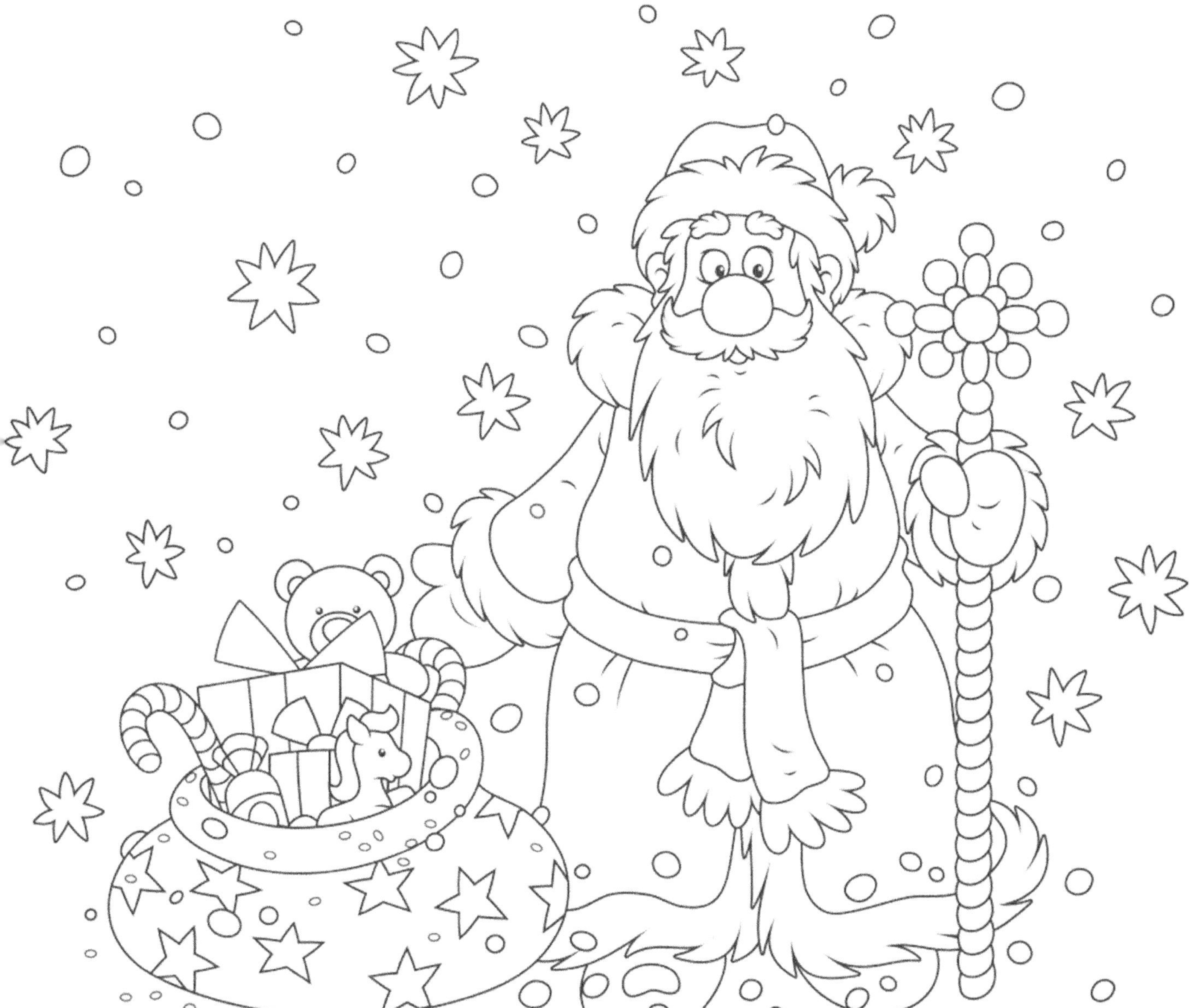

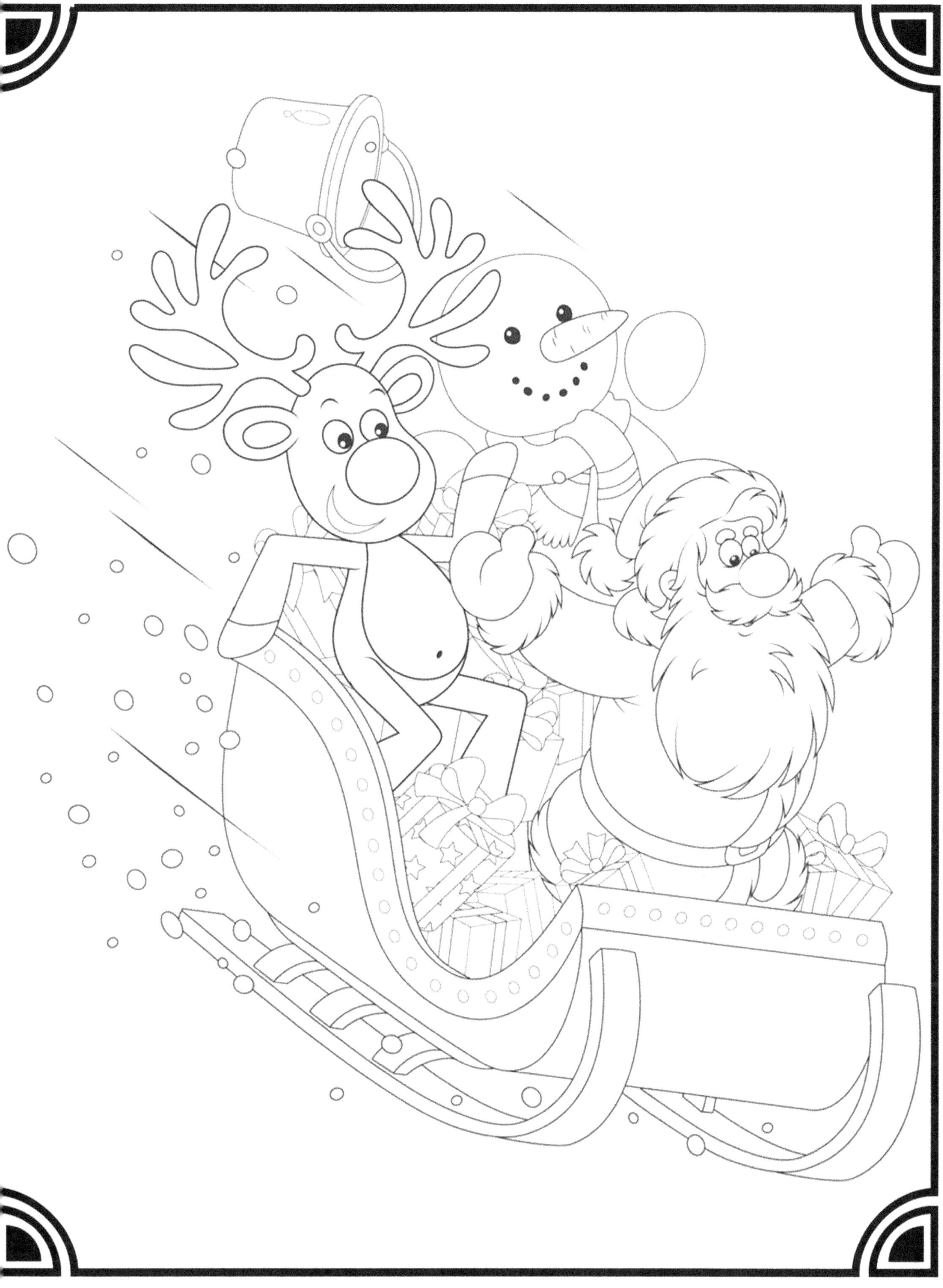

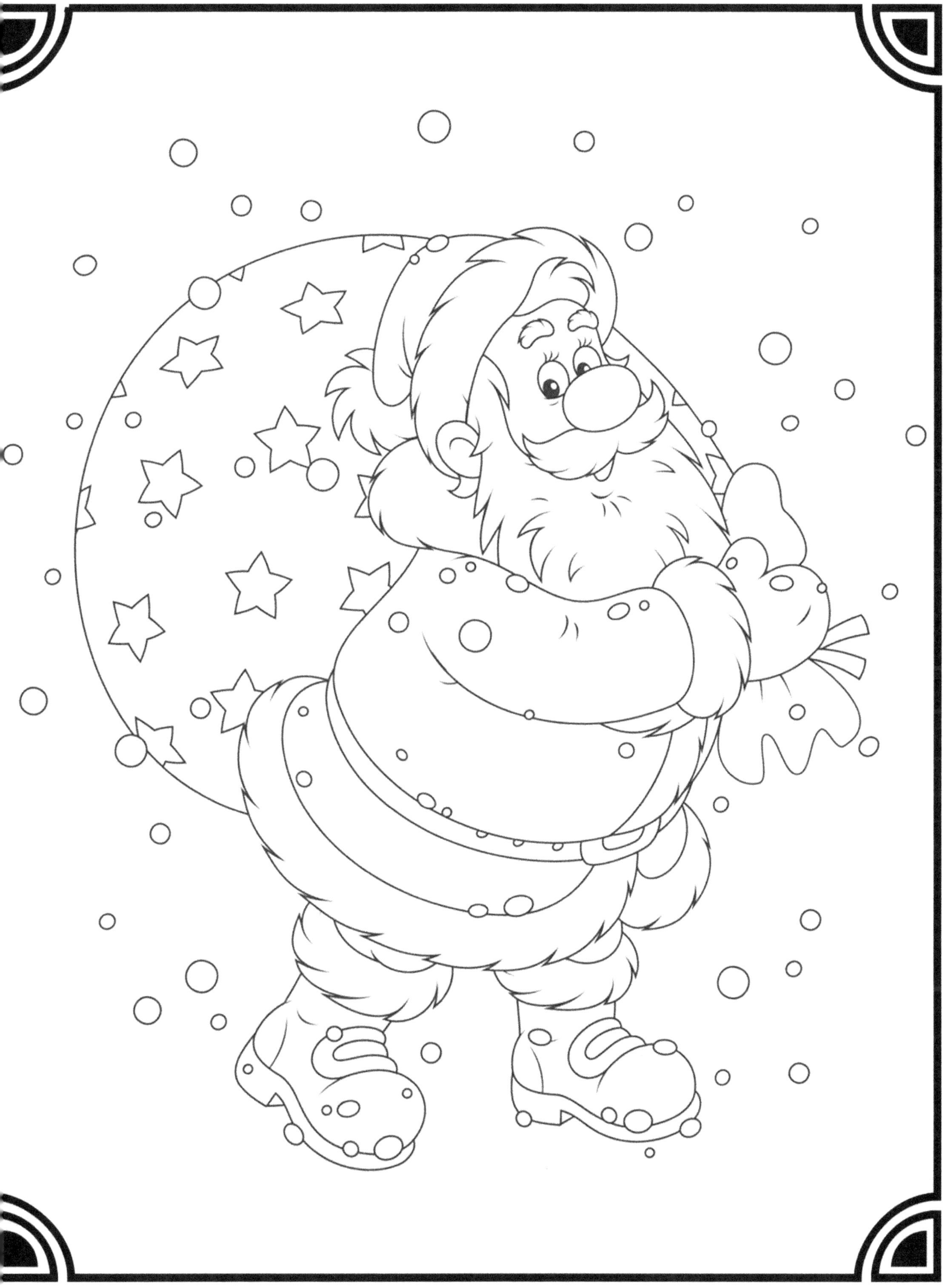

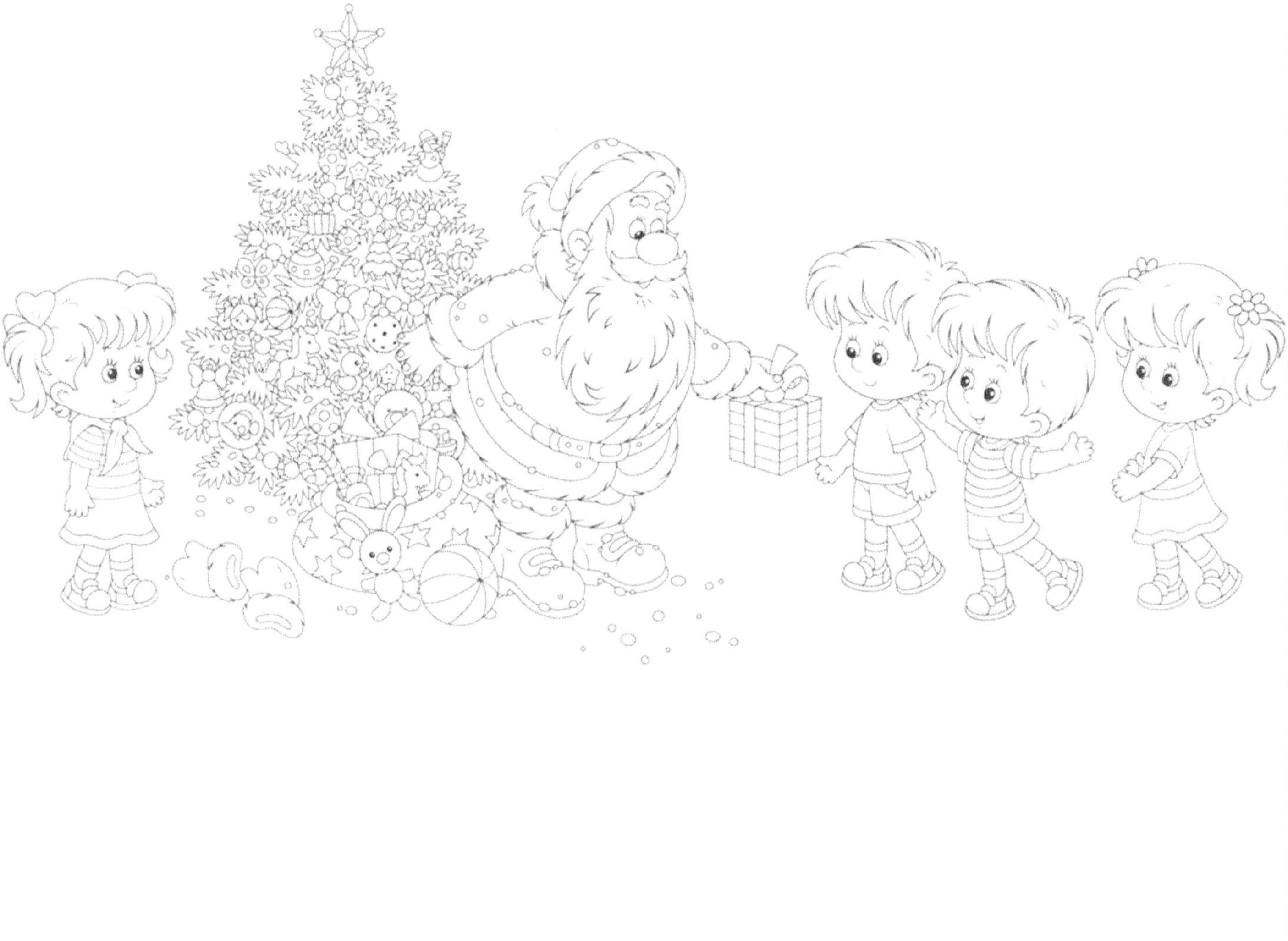

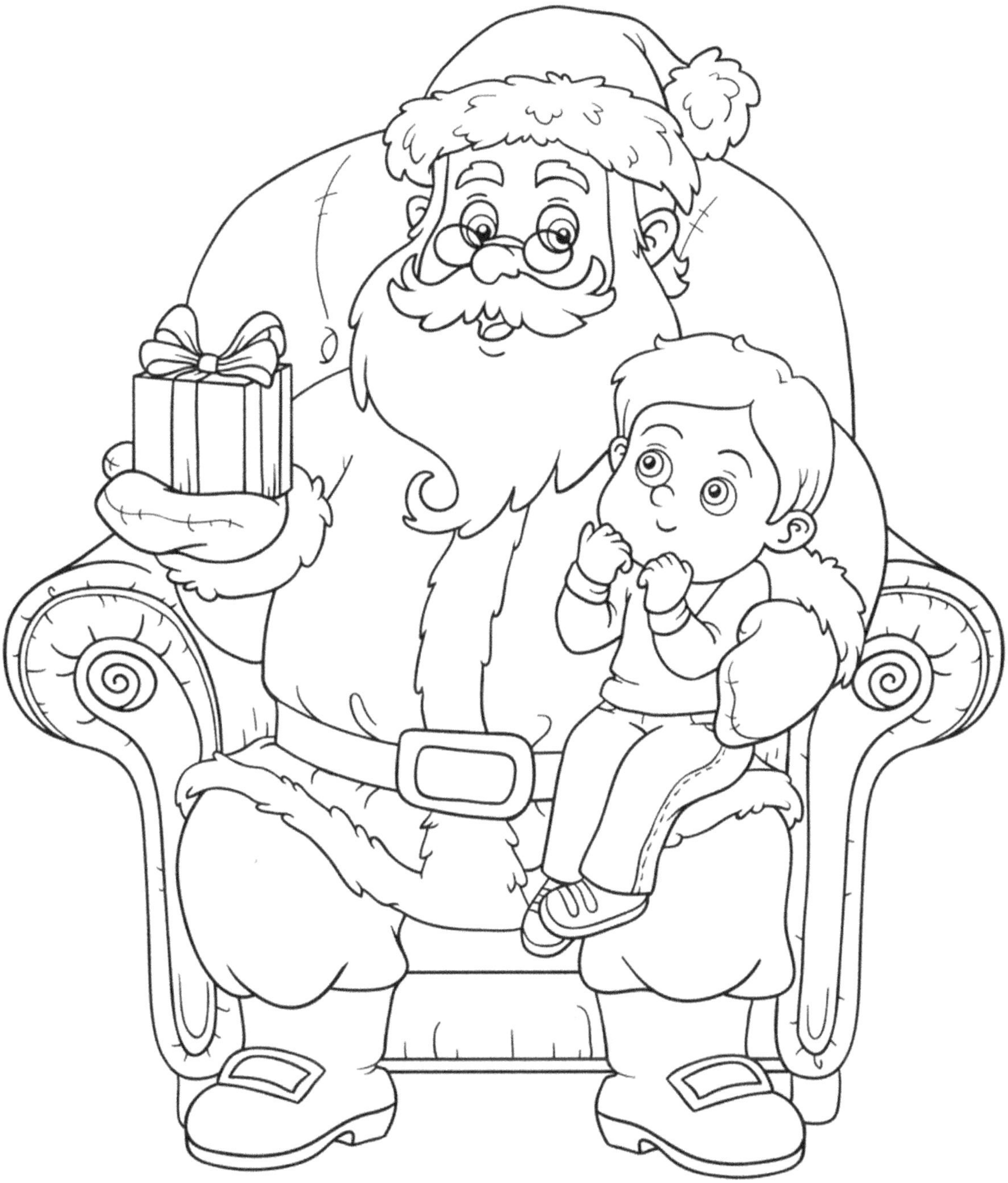

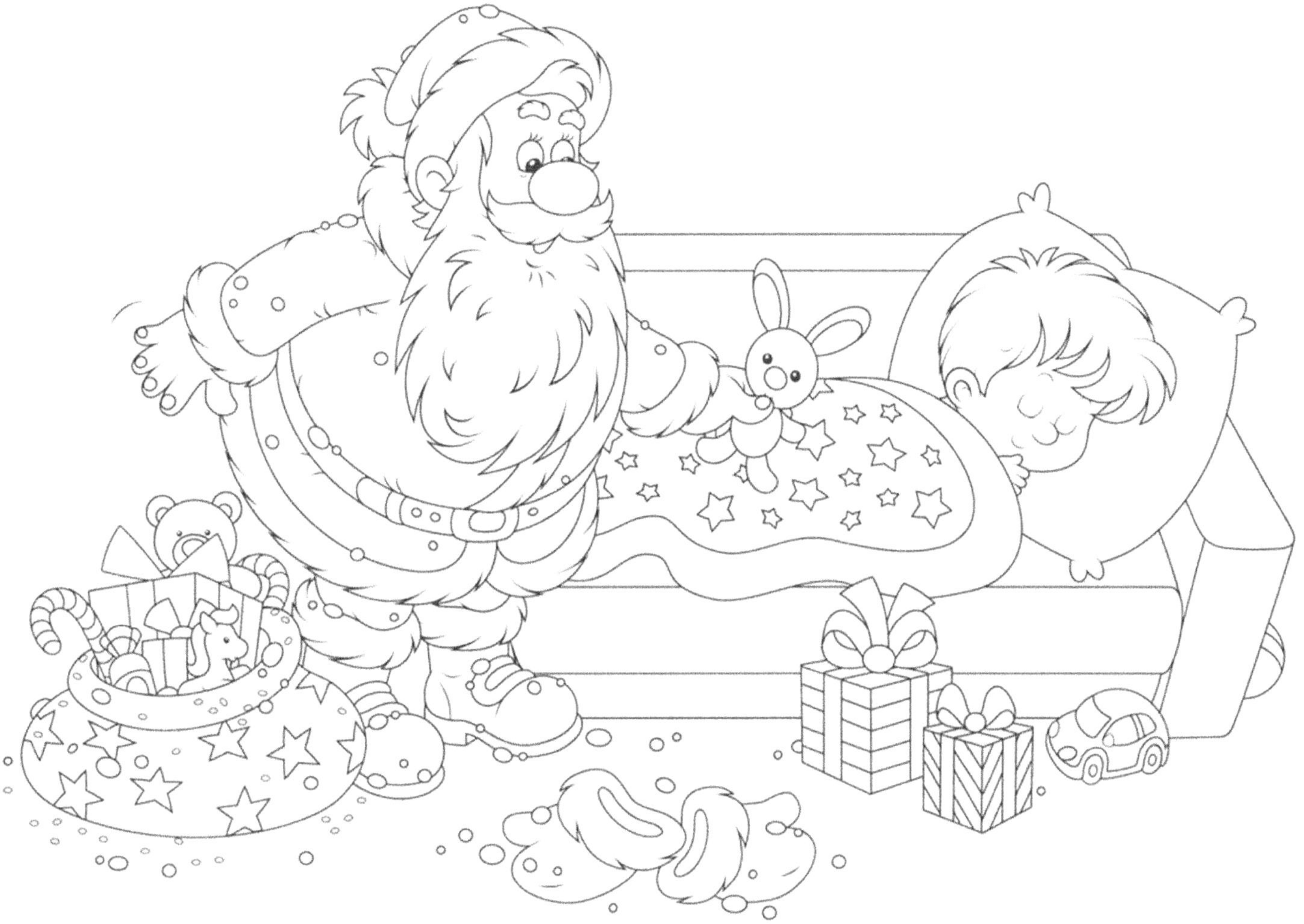

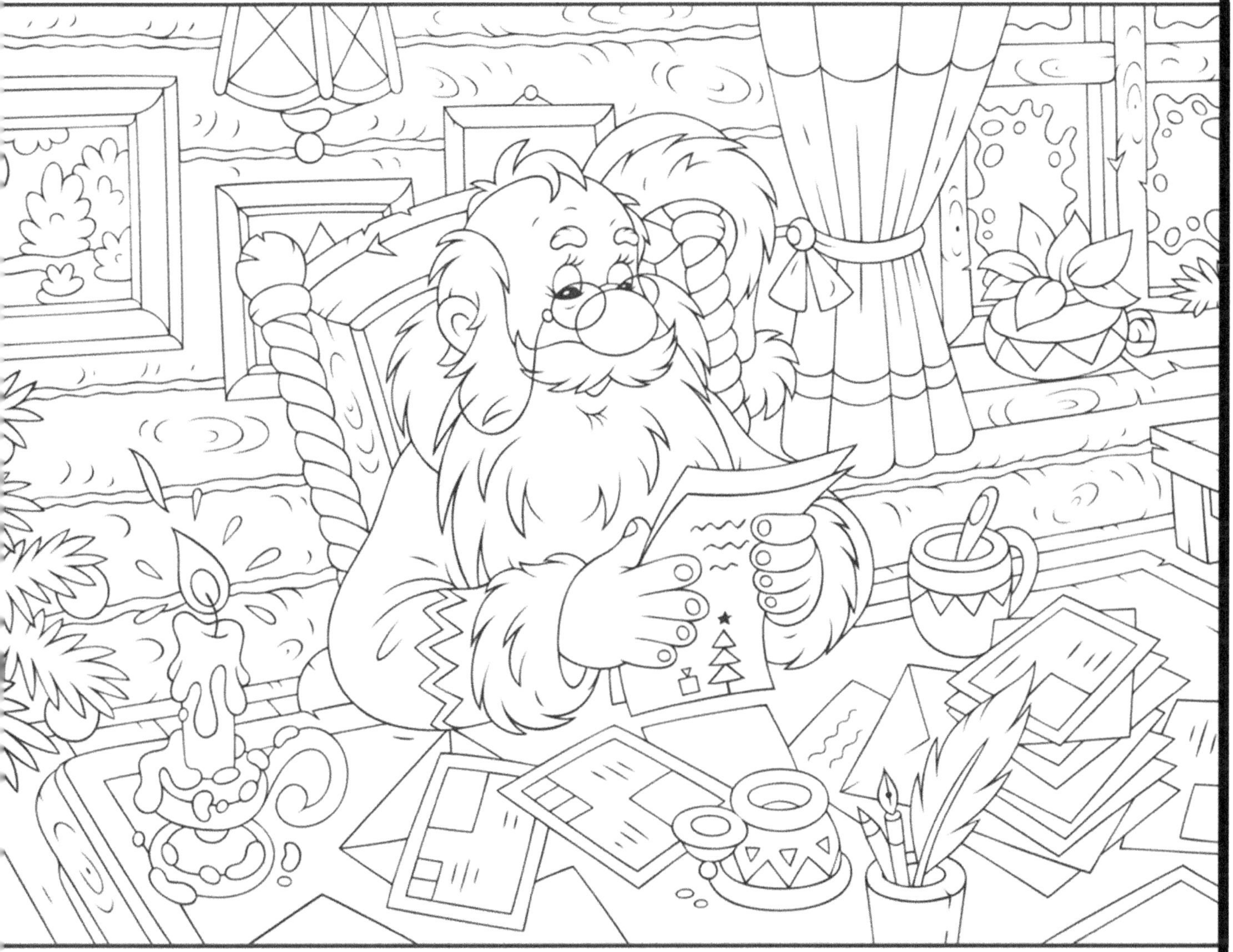

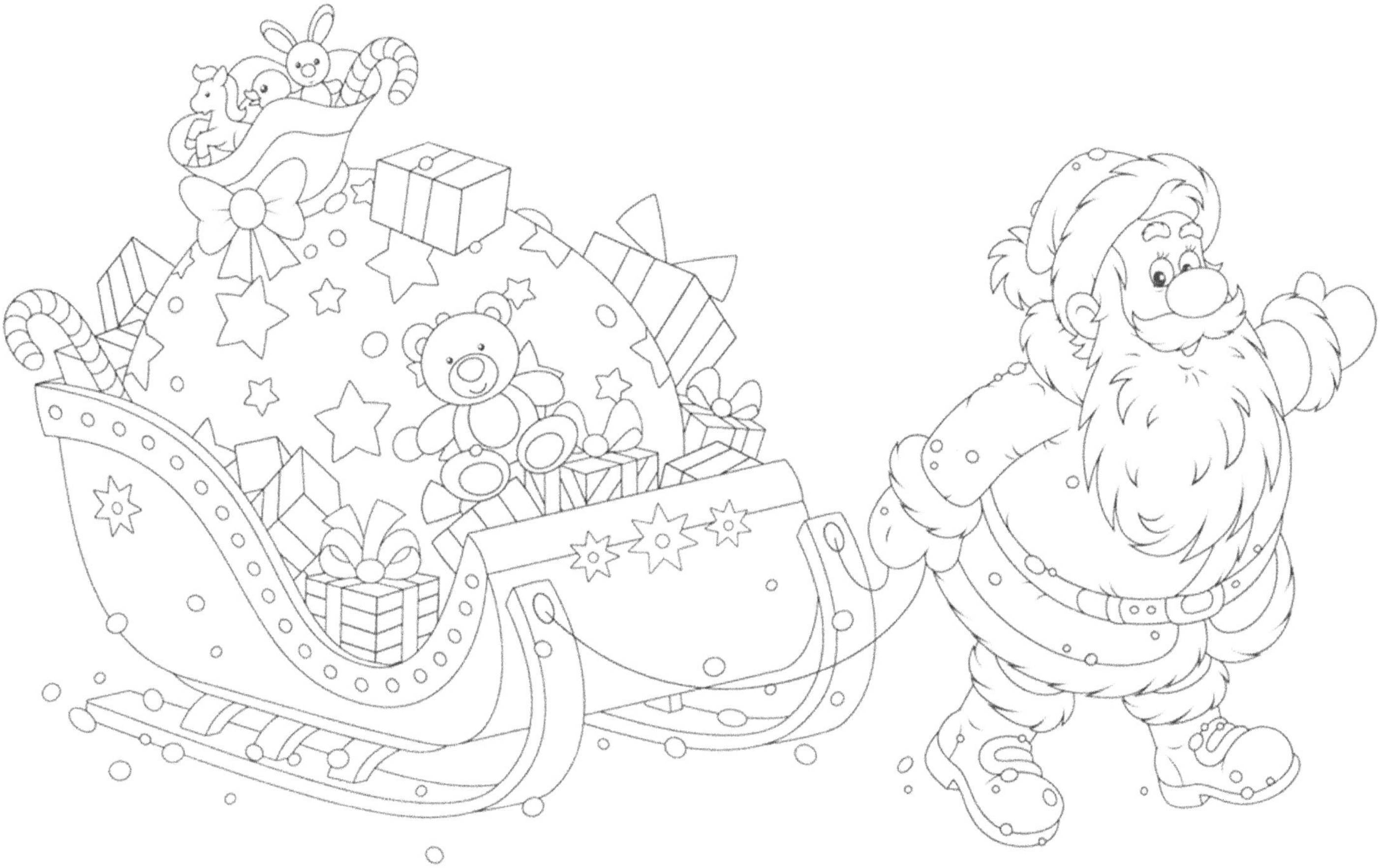

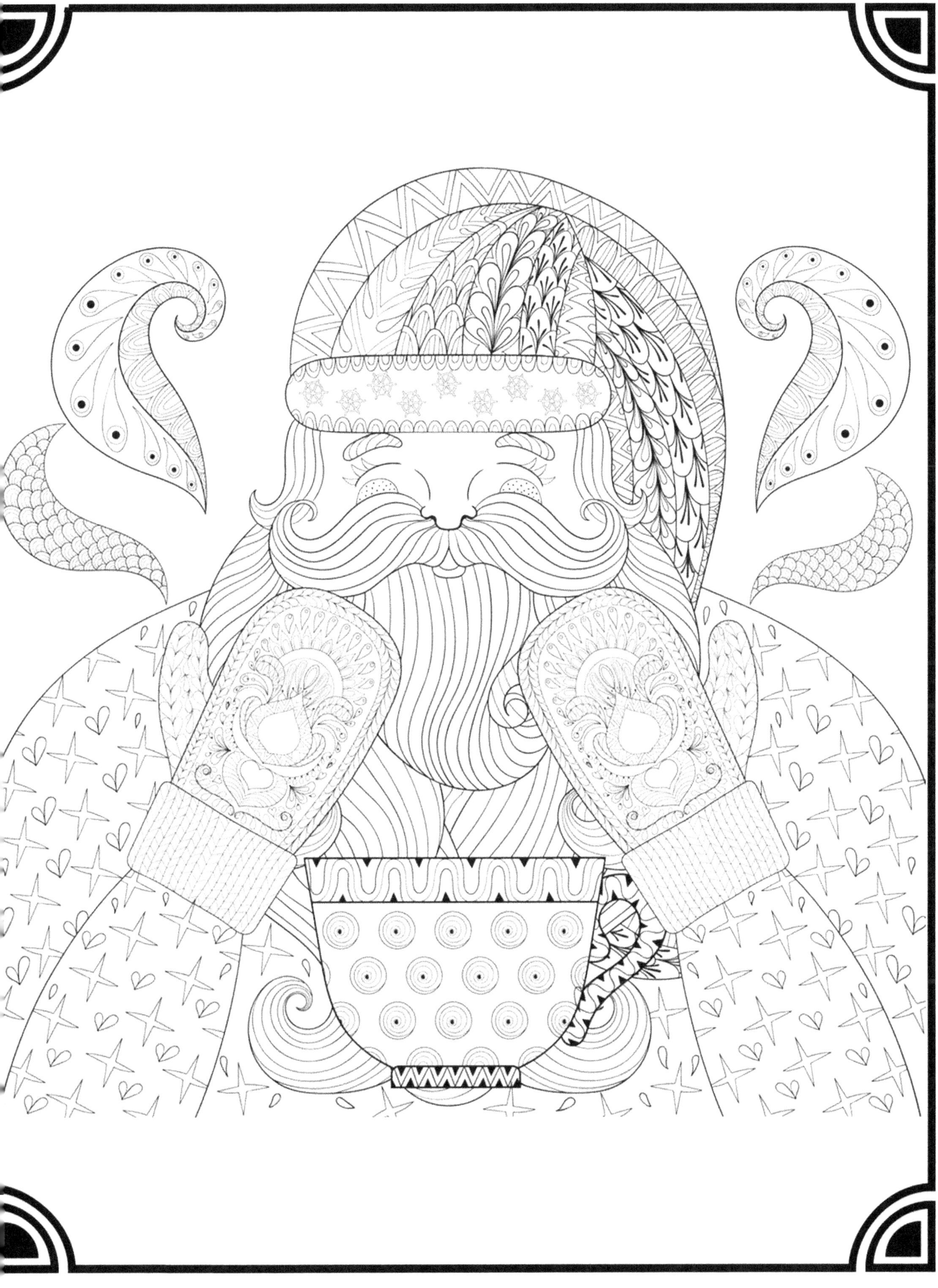

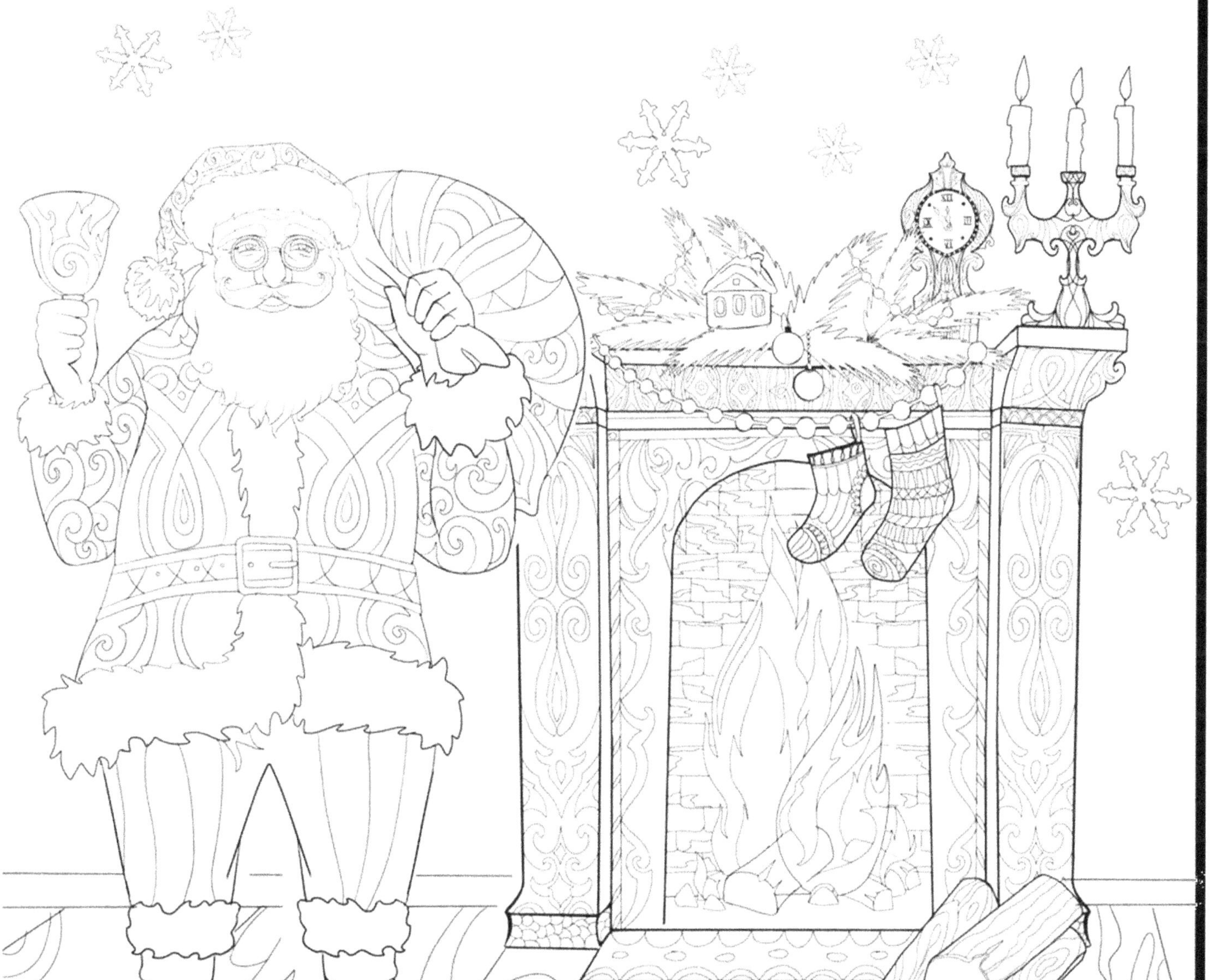

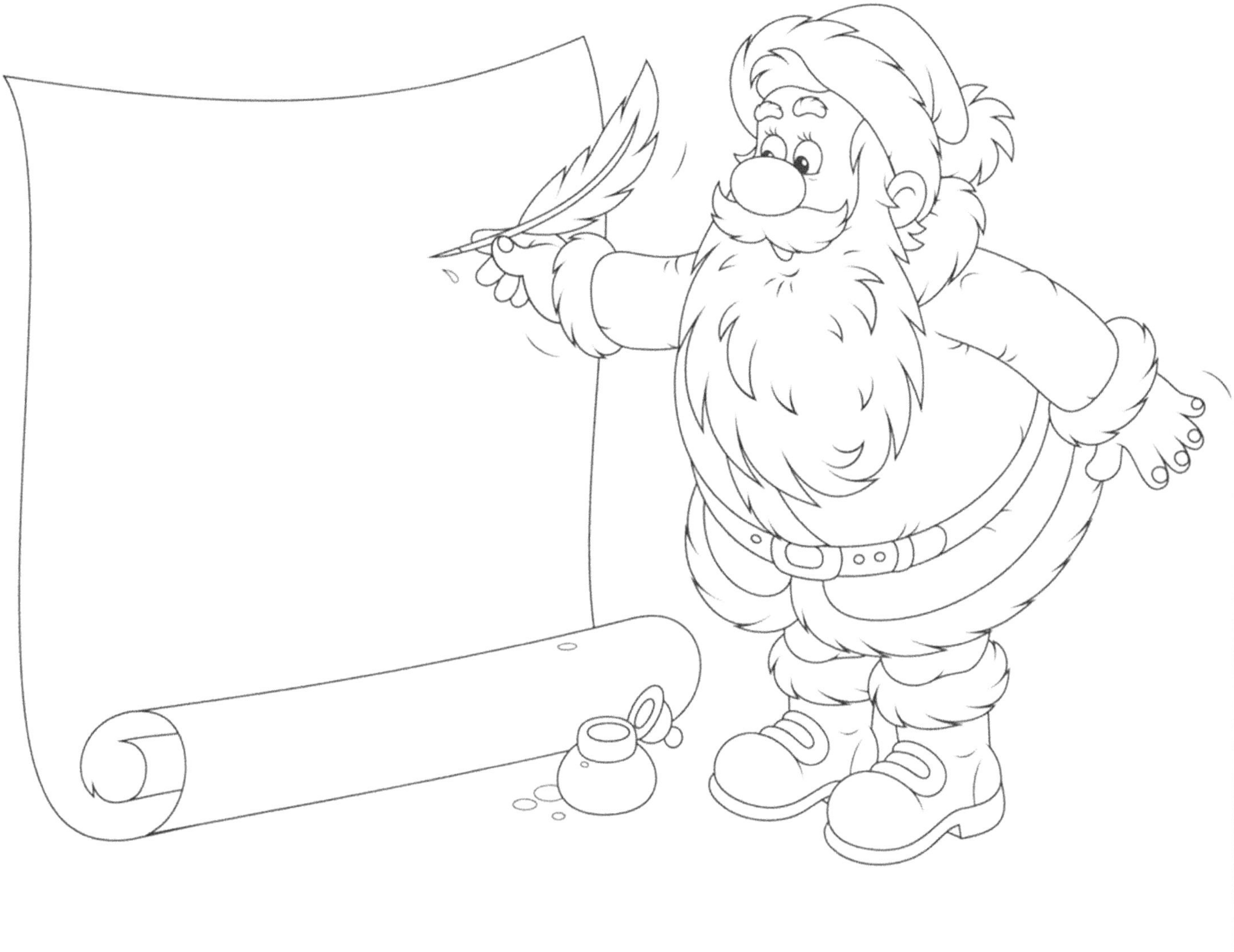

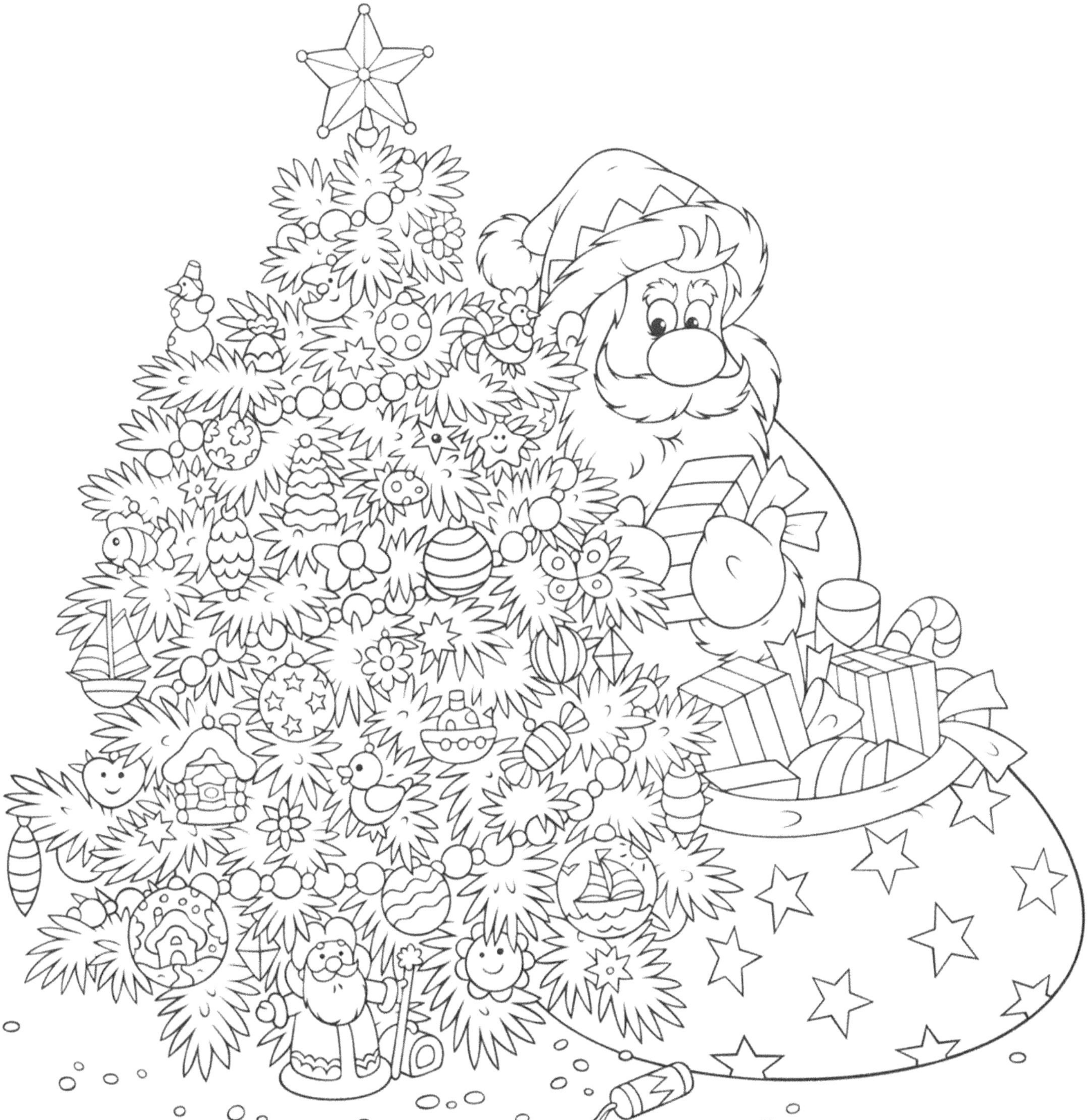

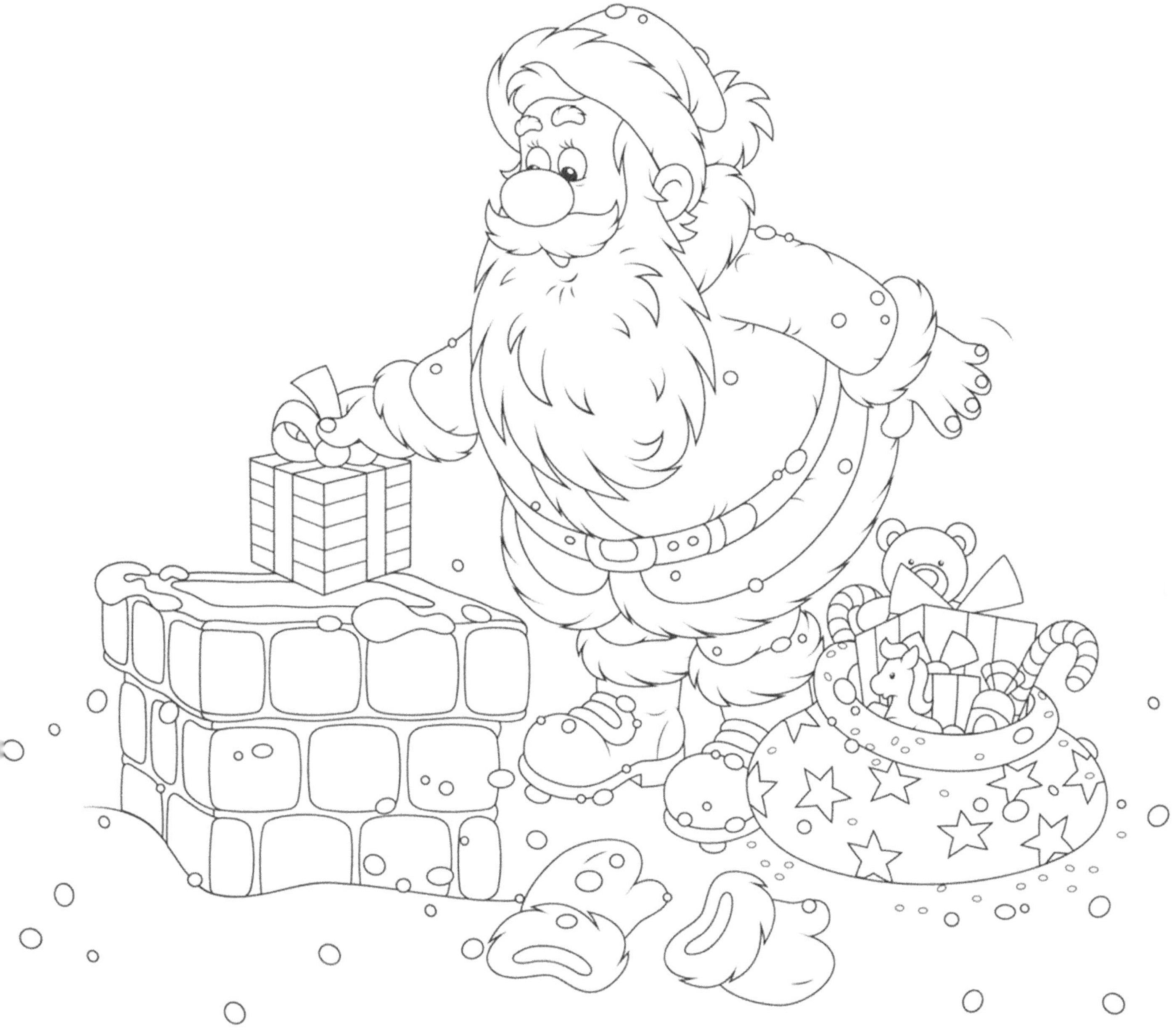

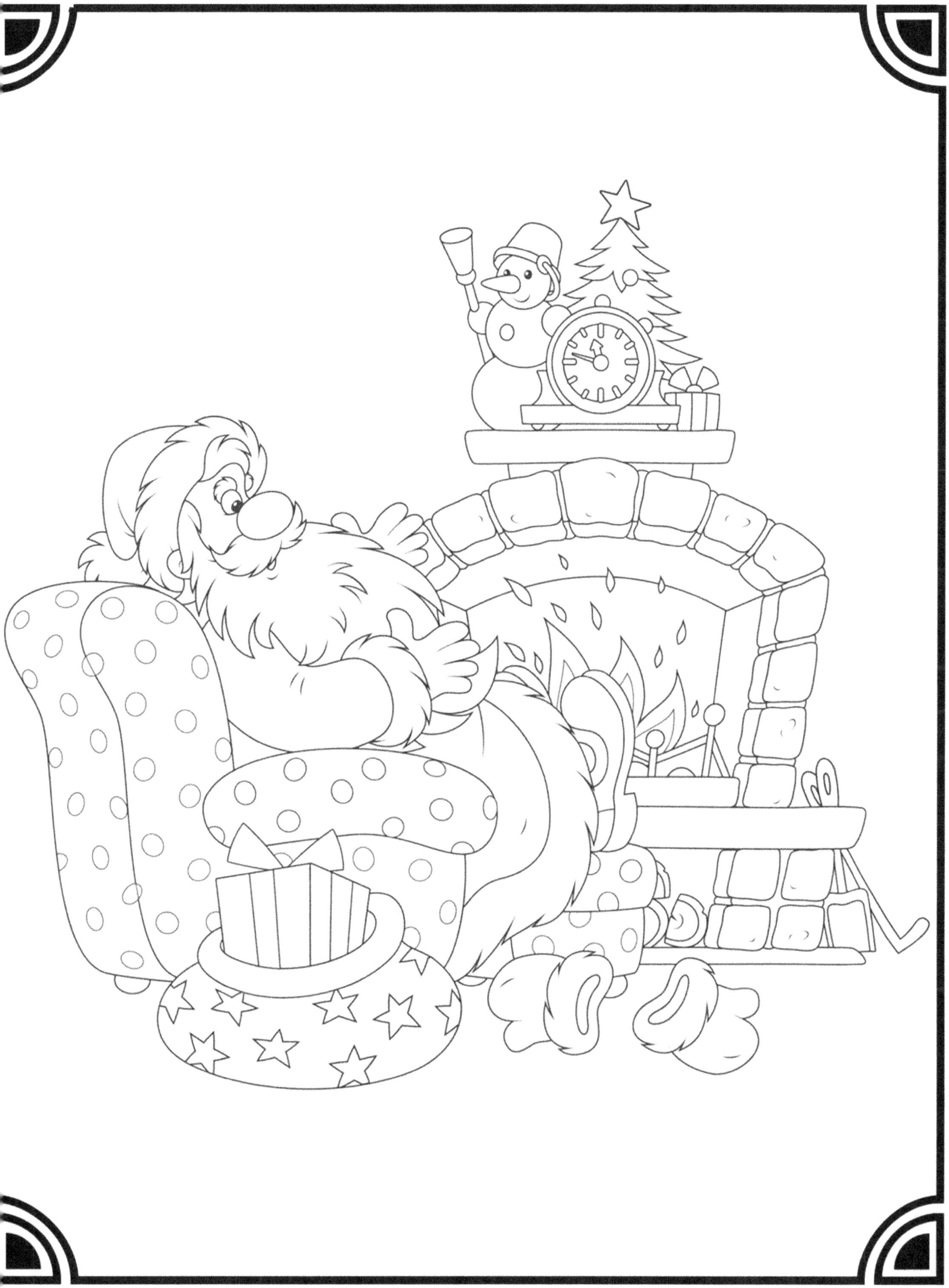

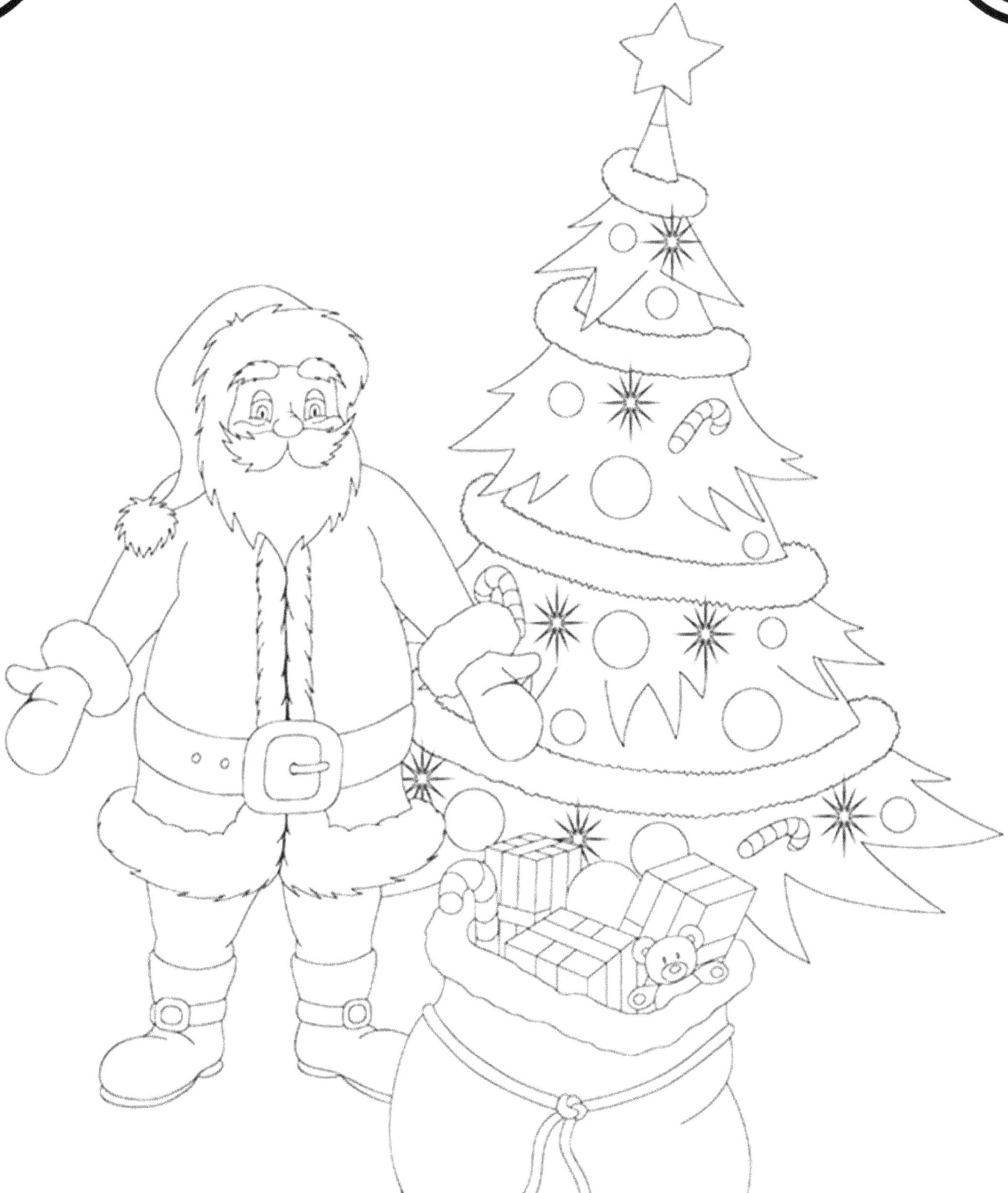

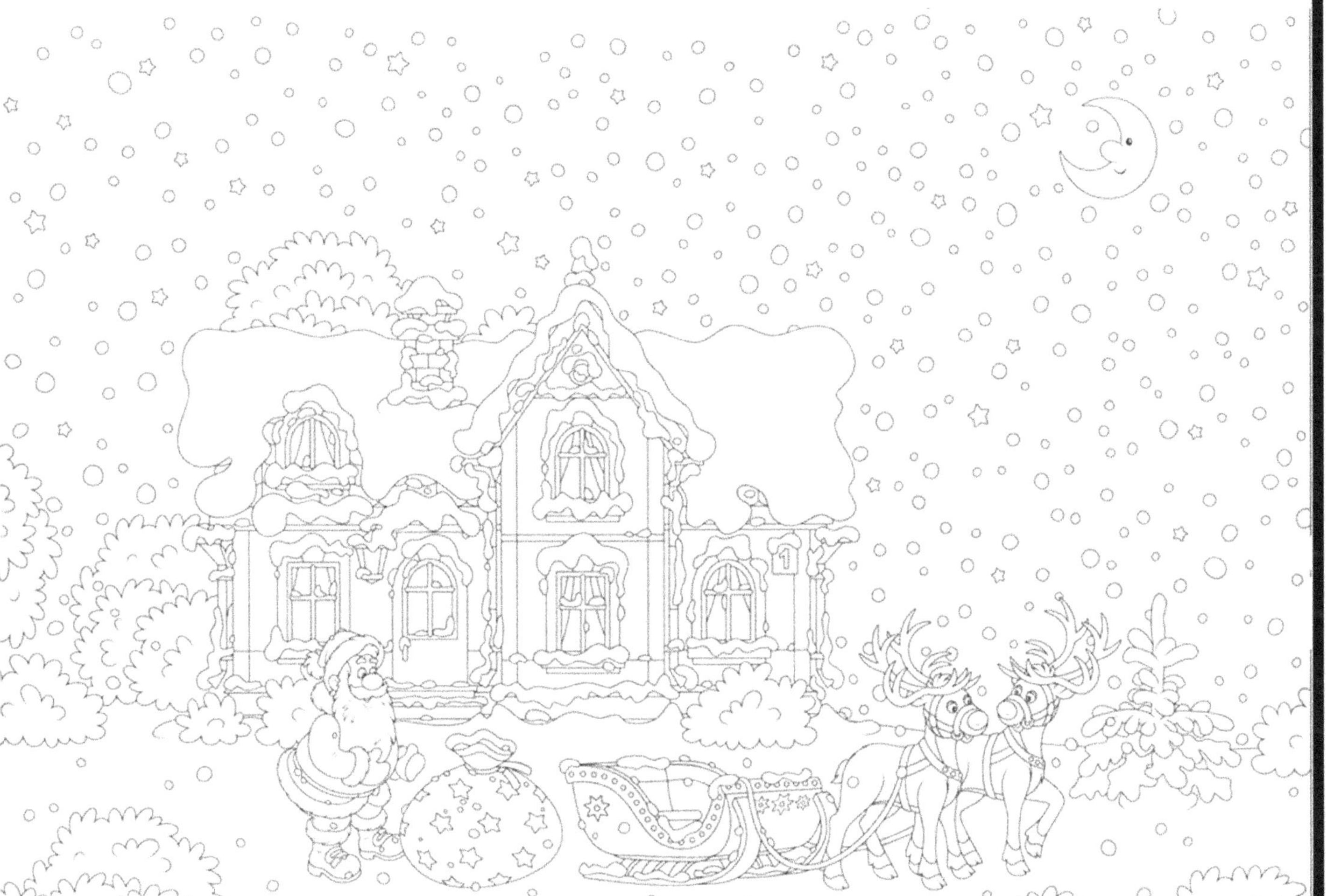

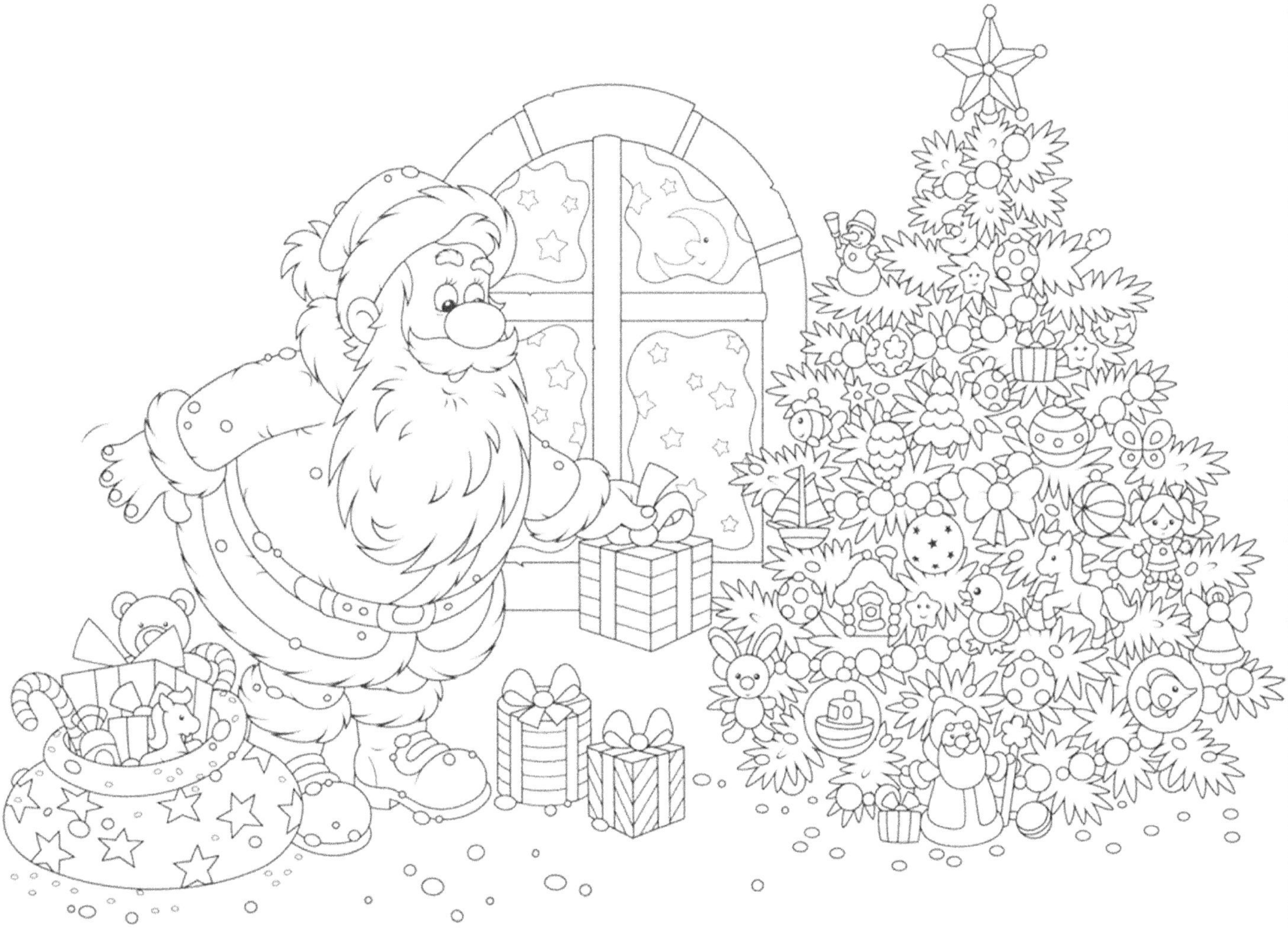

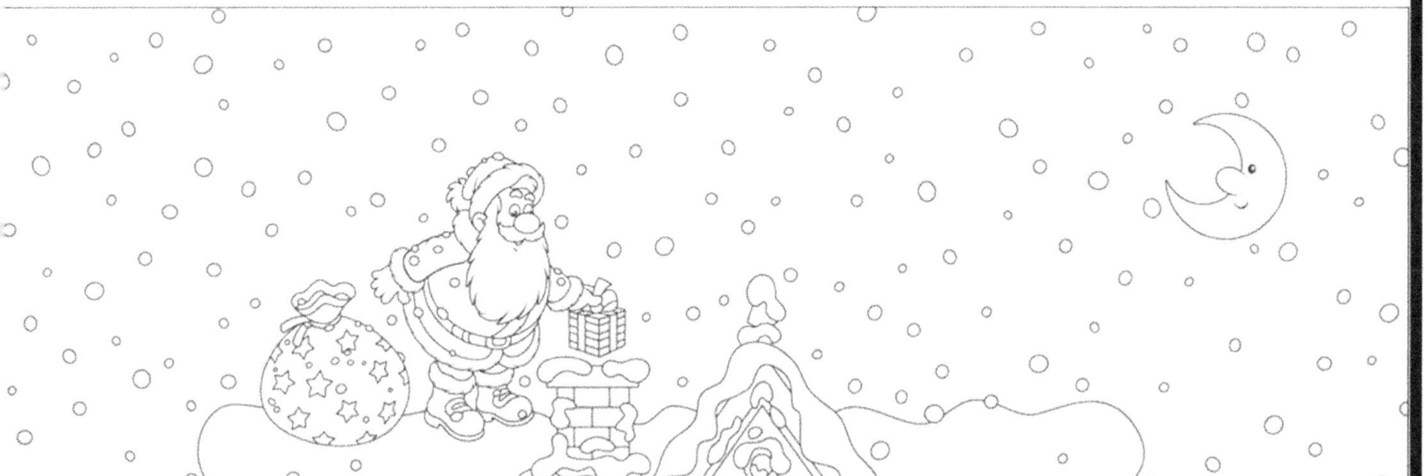
1

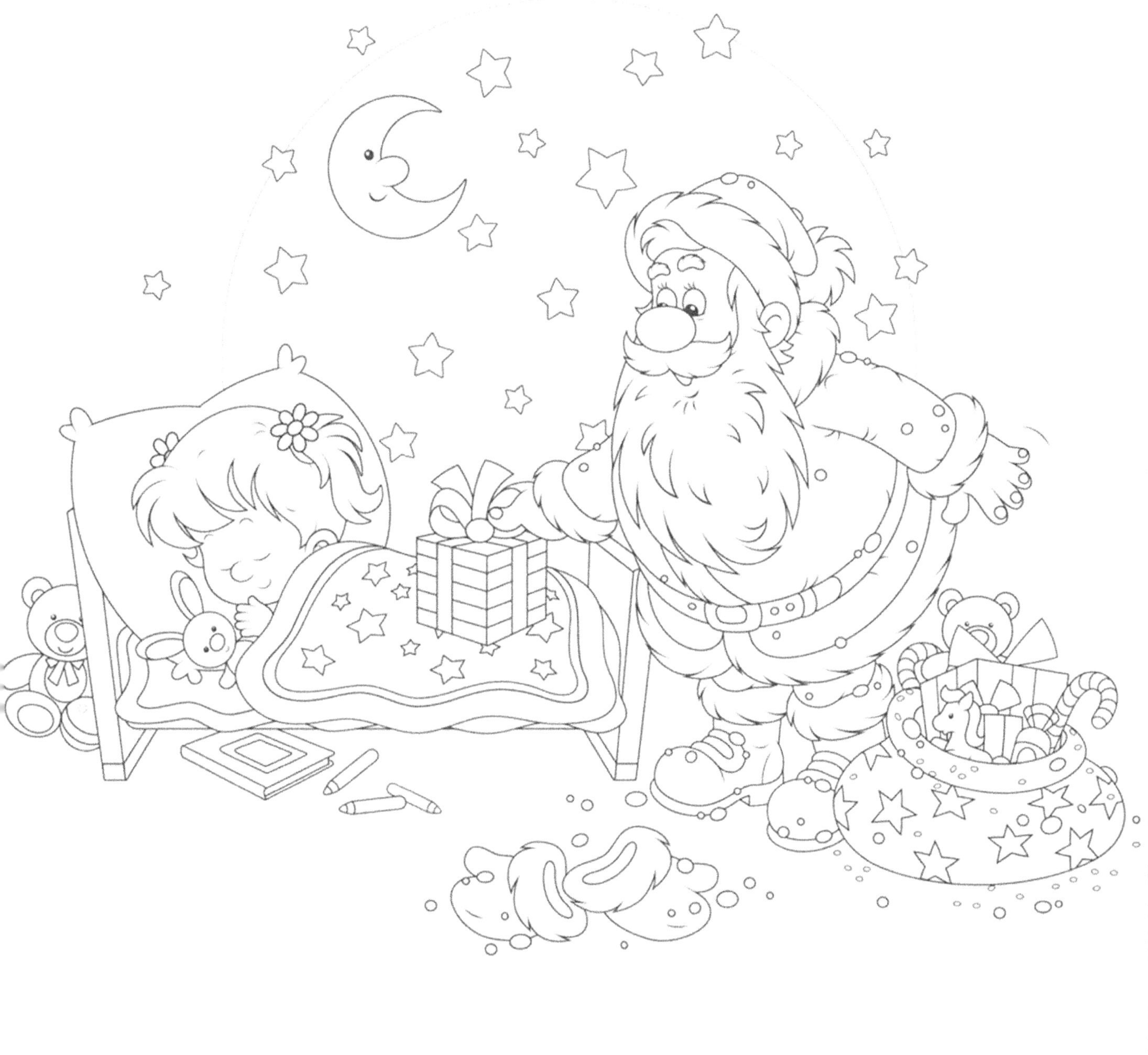

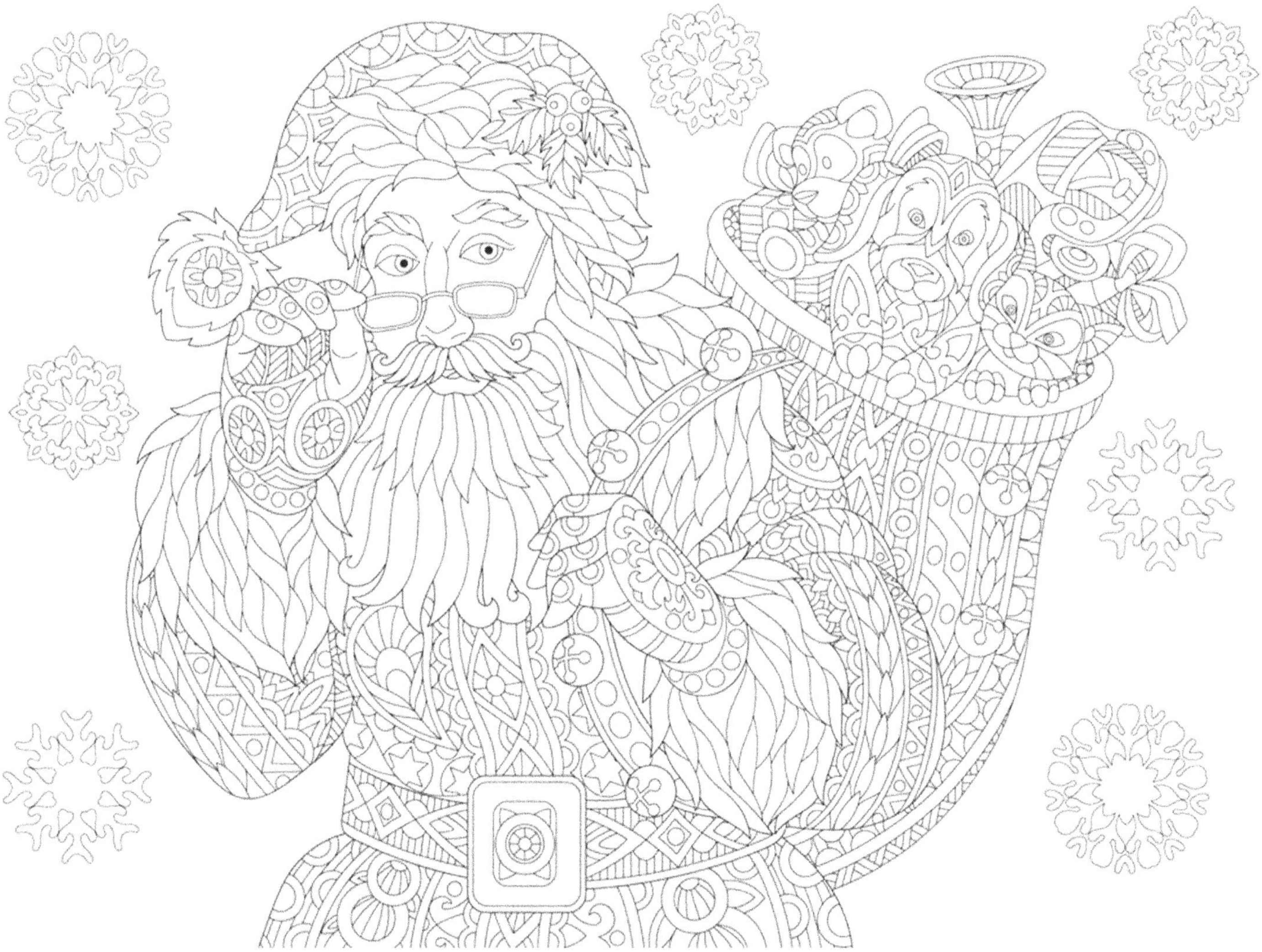

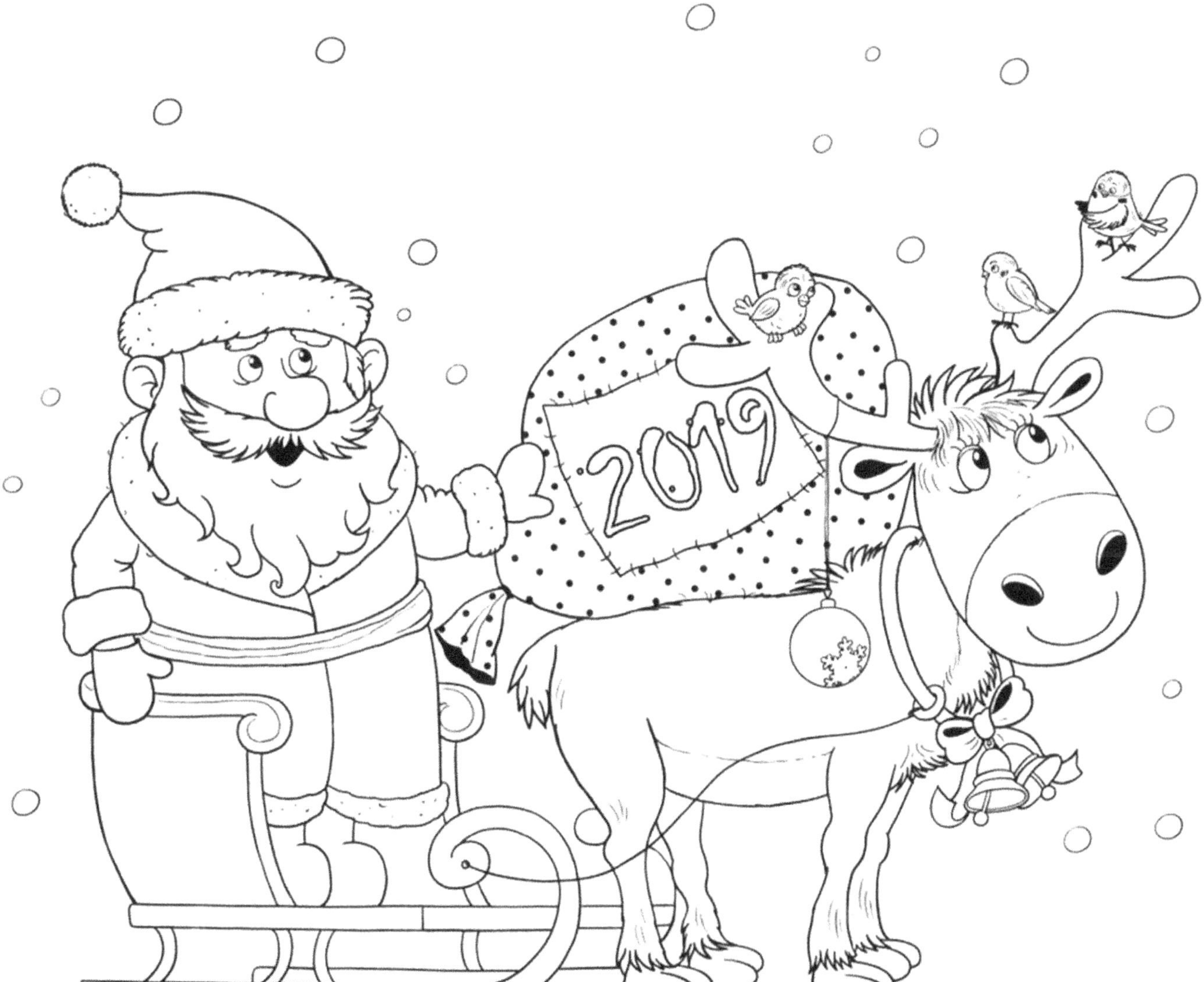
2019

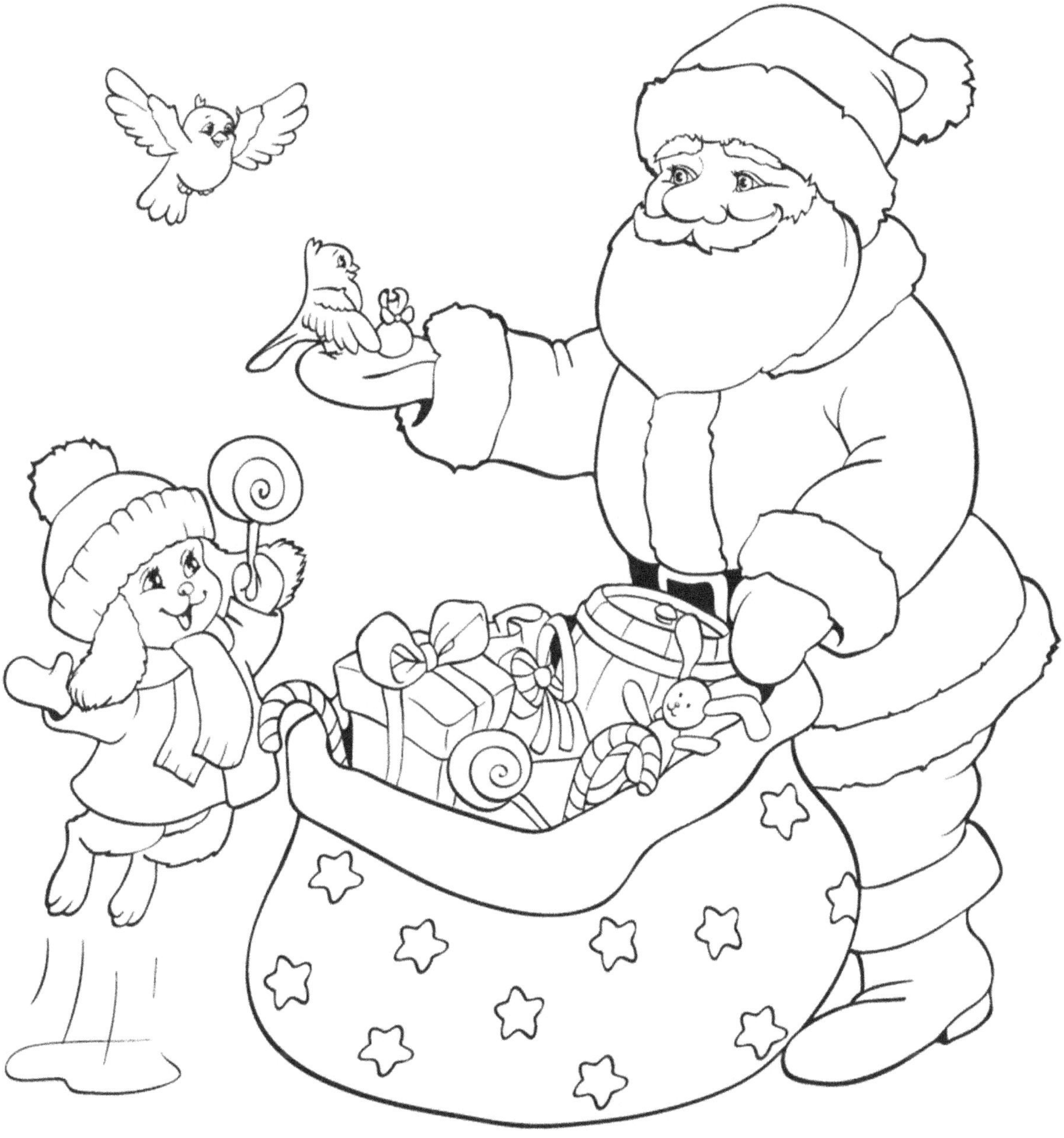

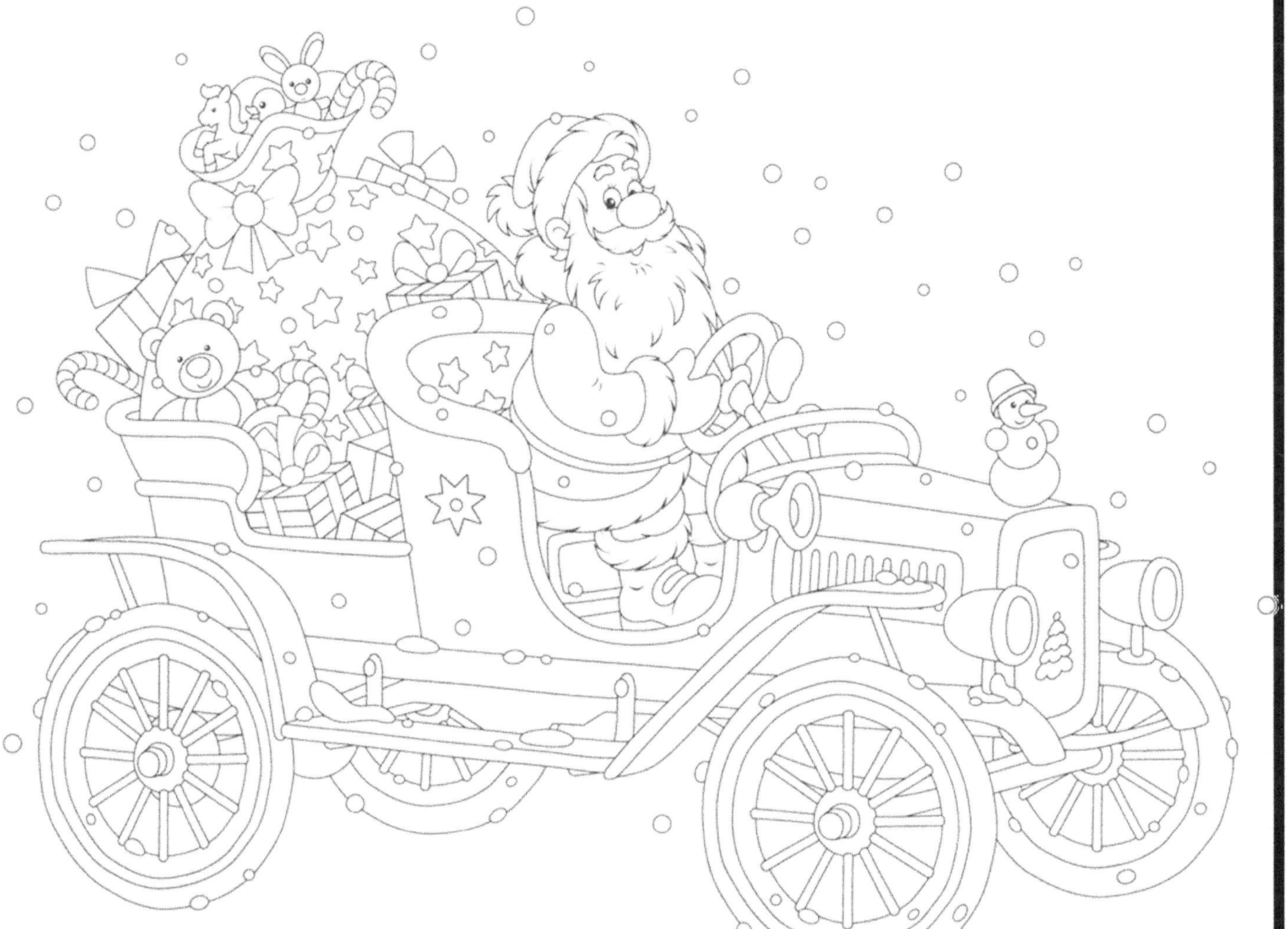

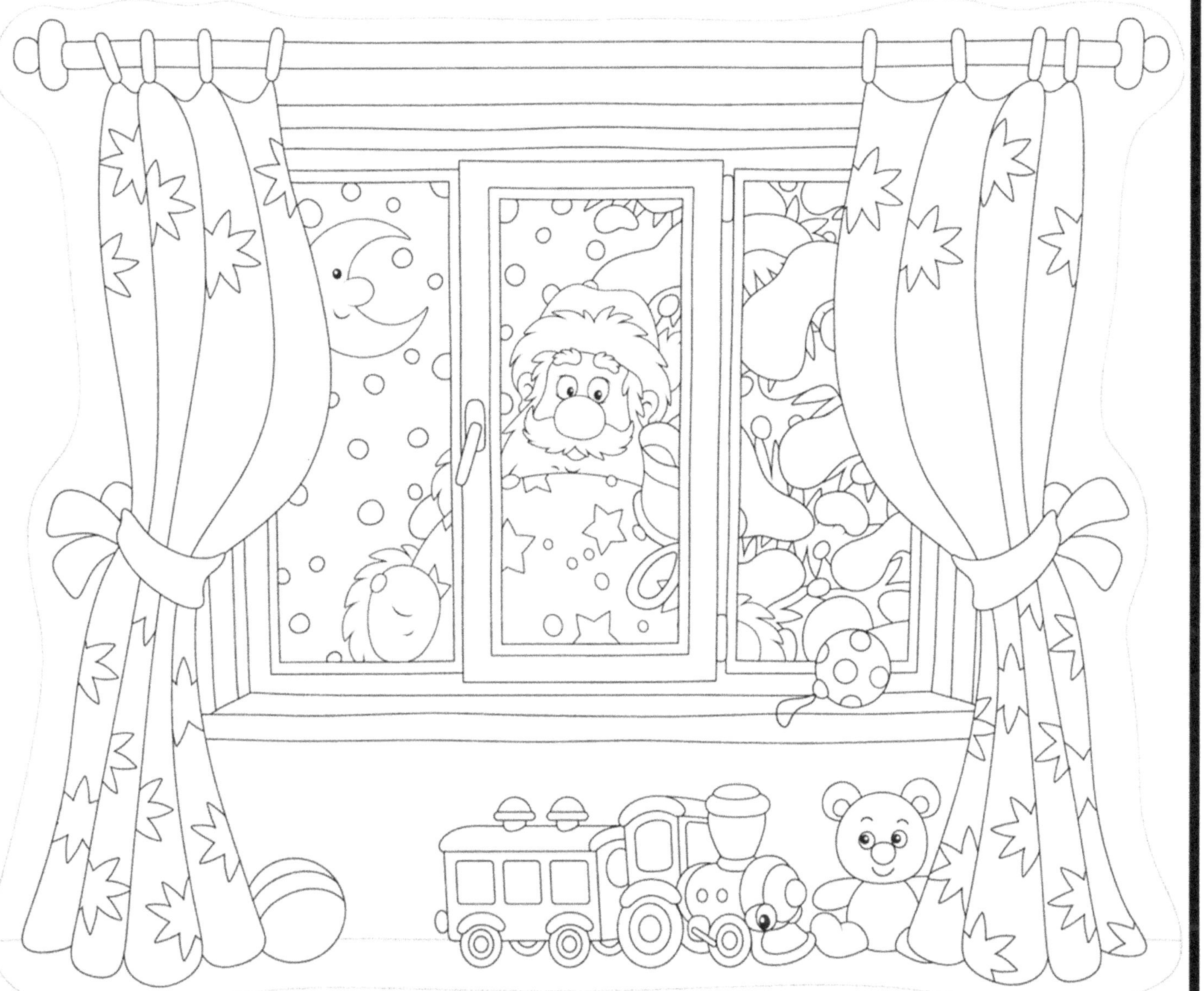

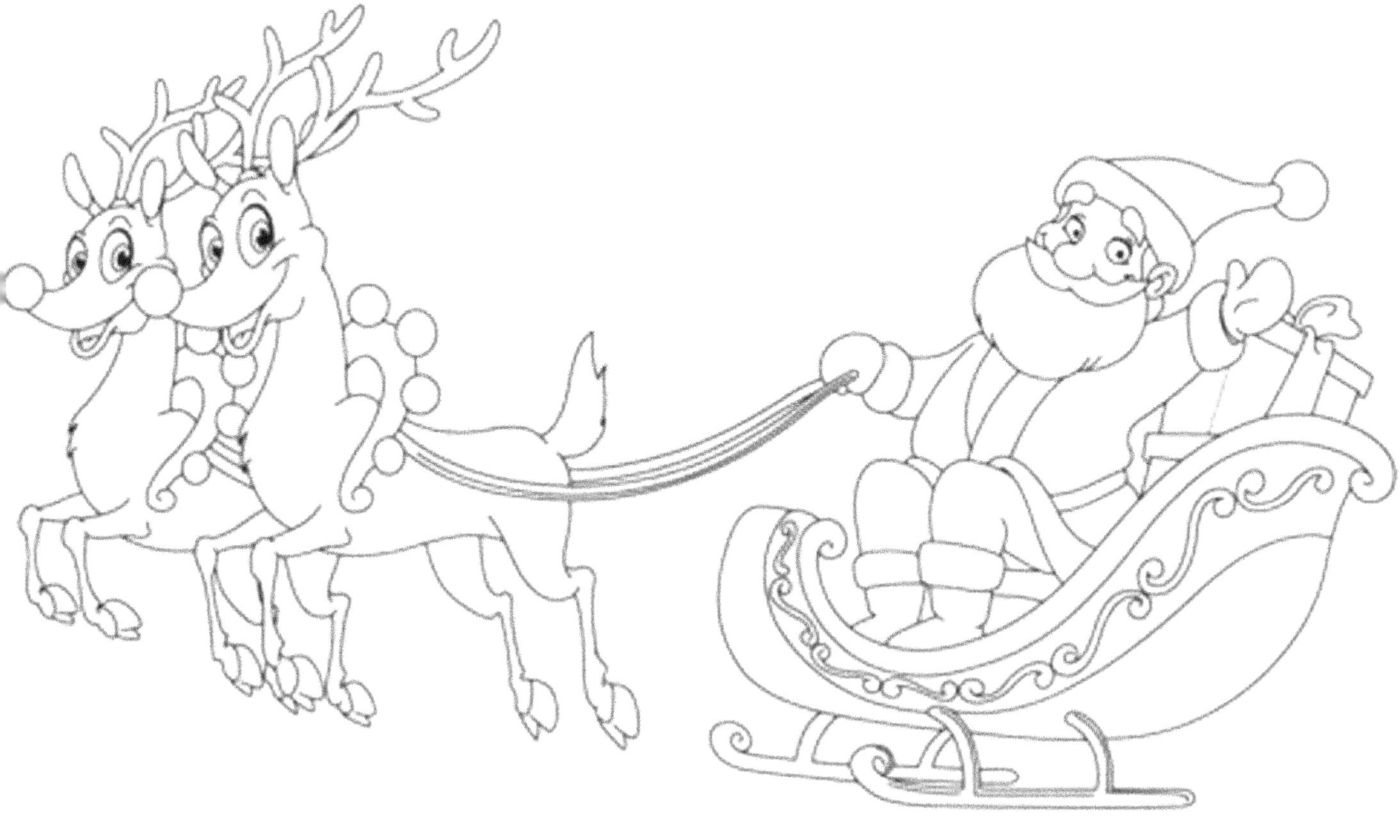

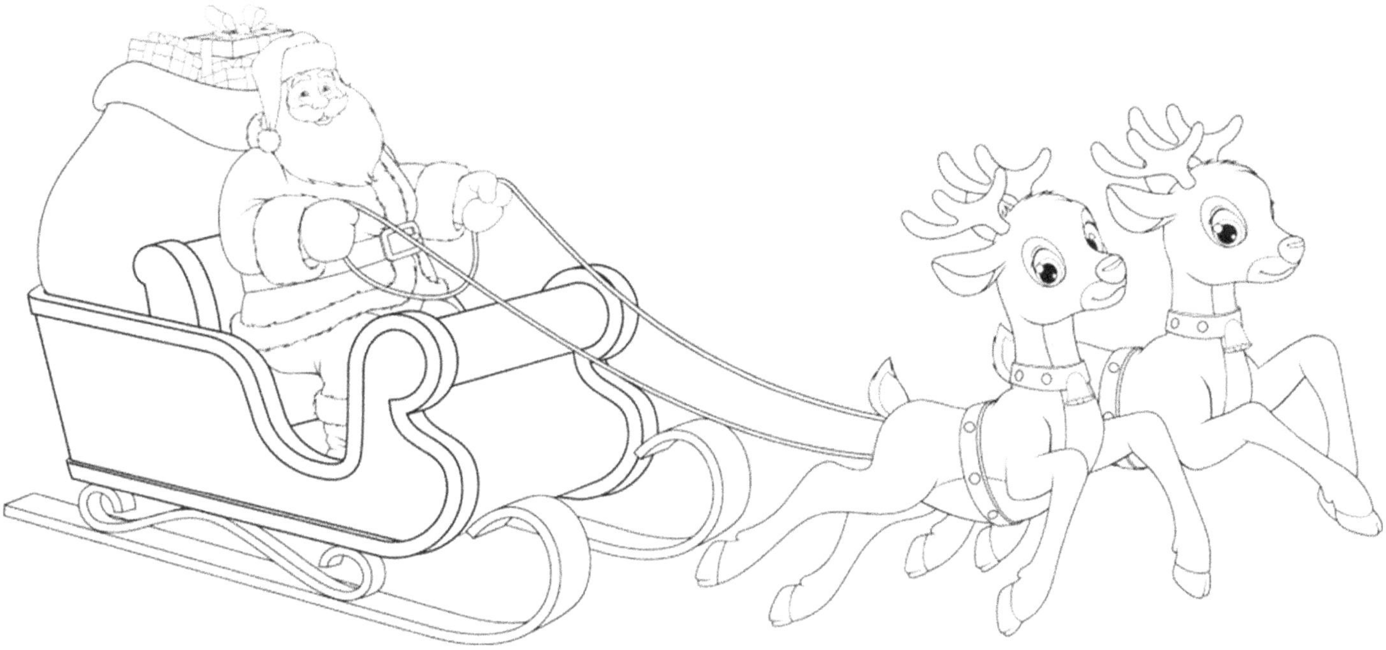

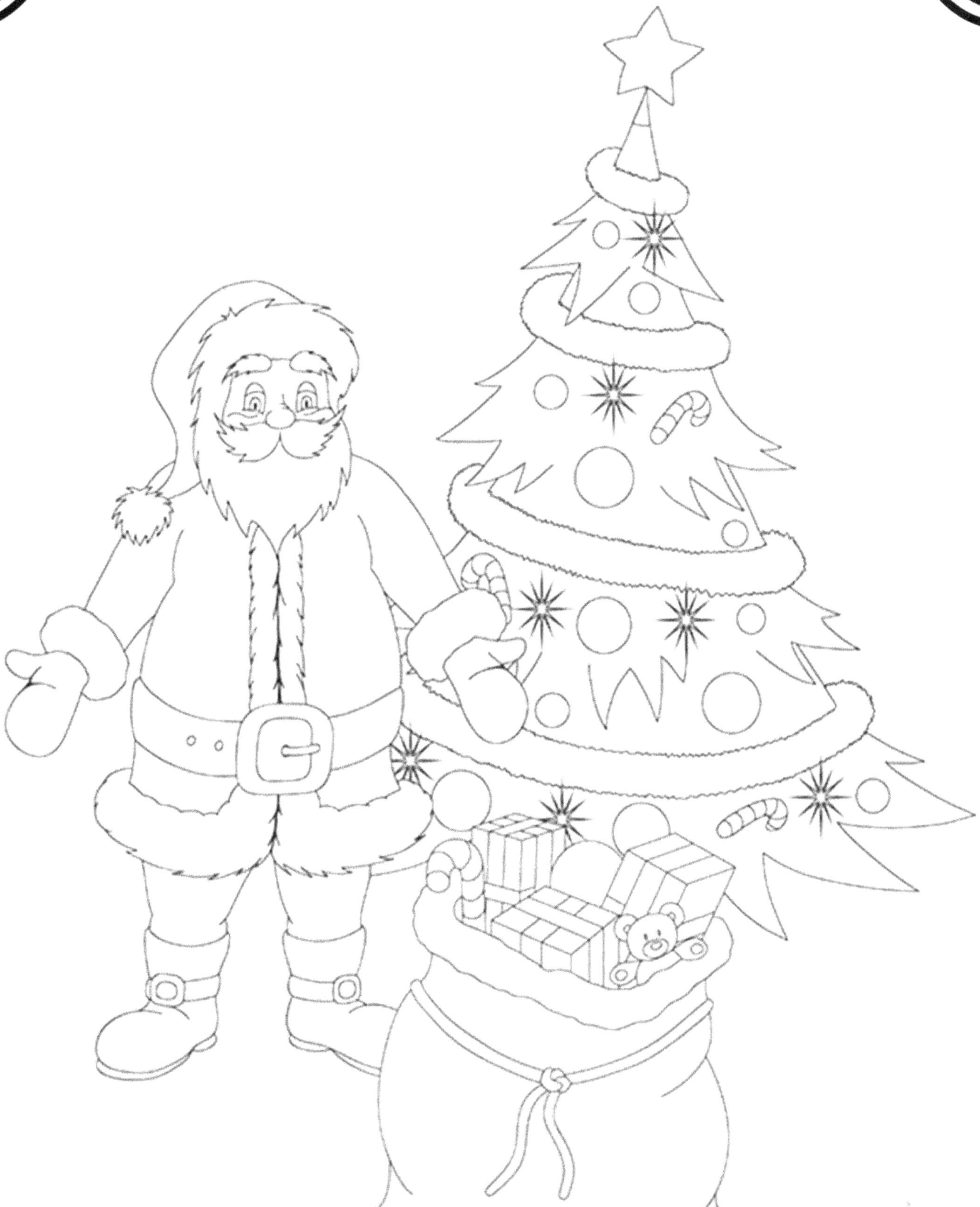

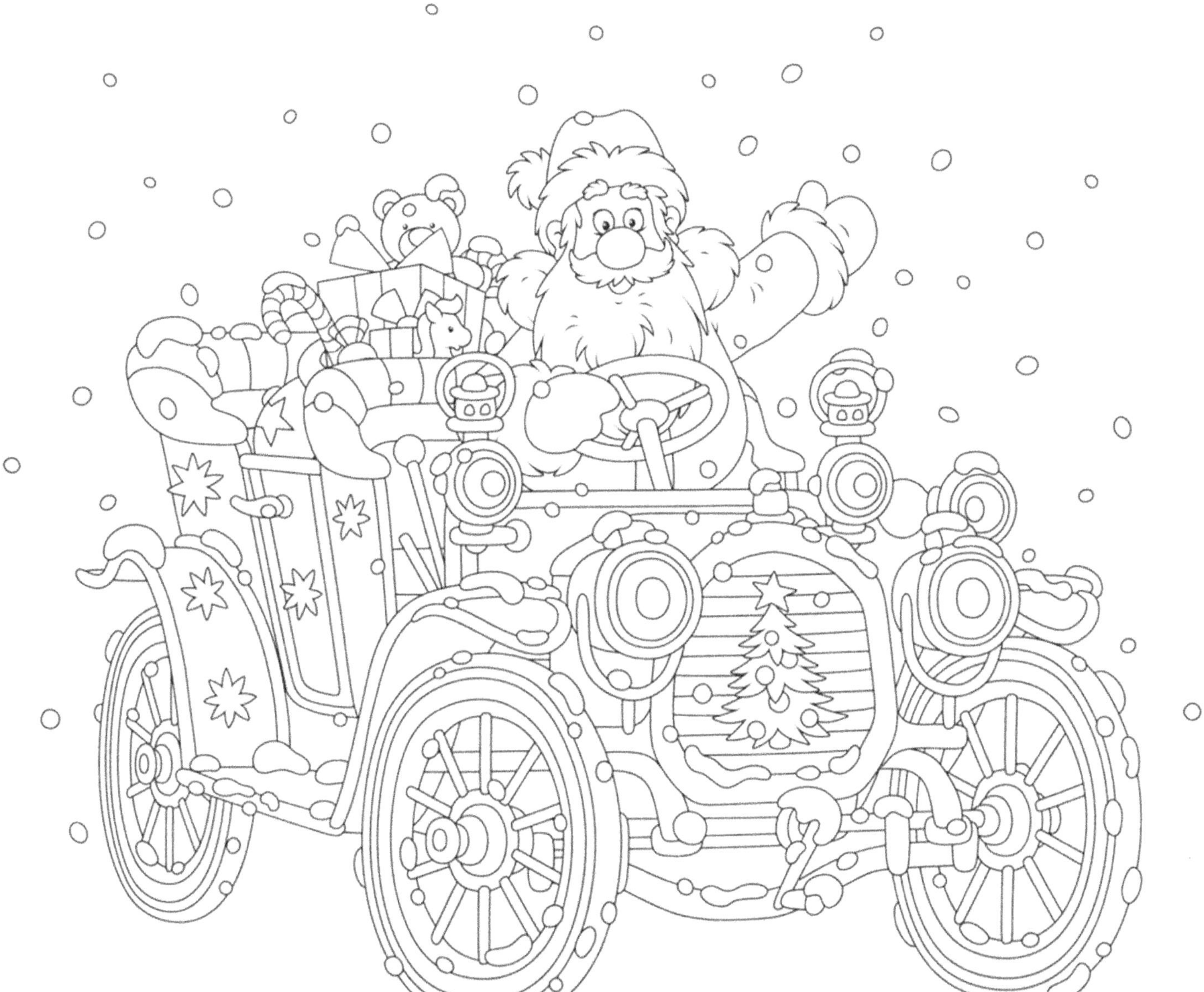

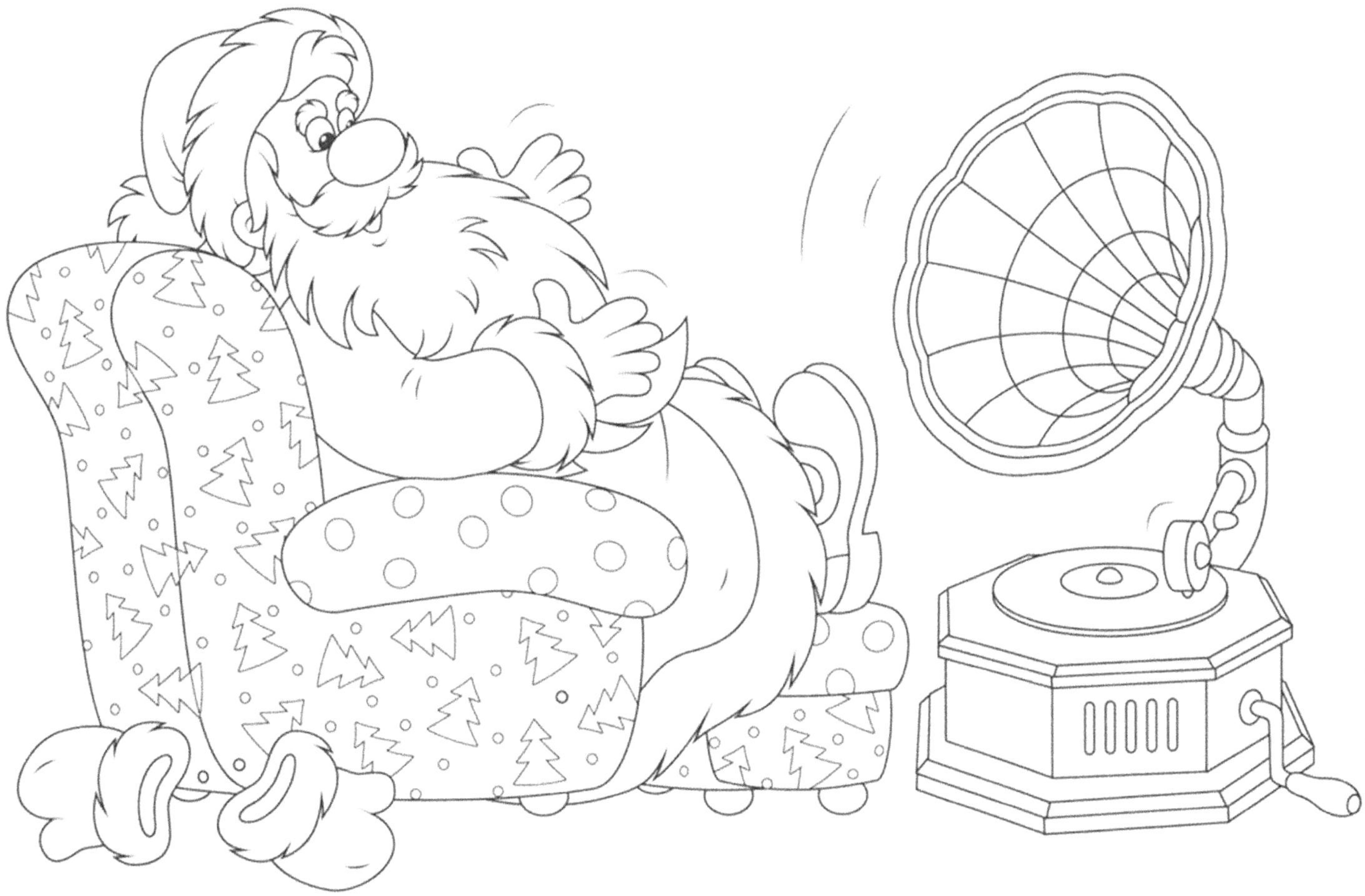

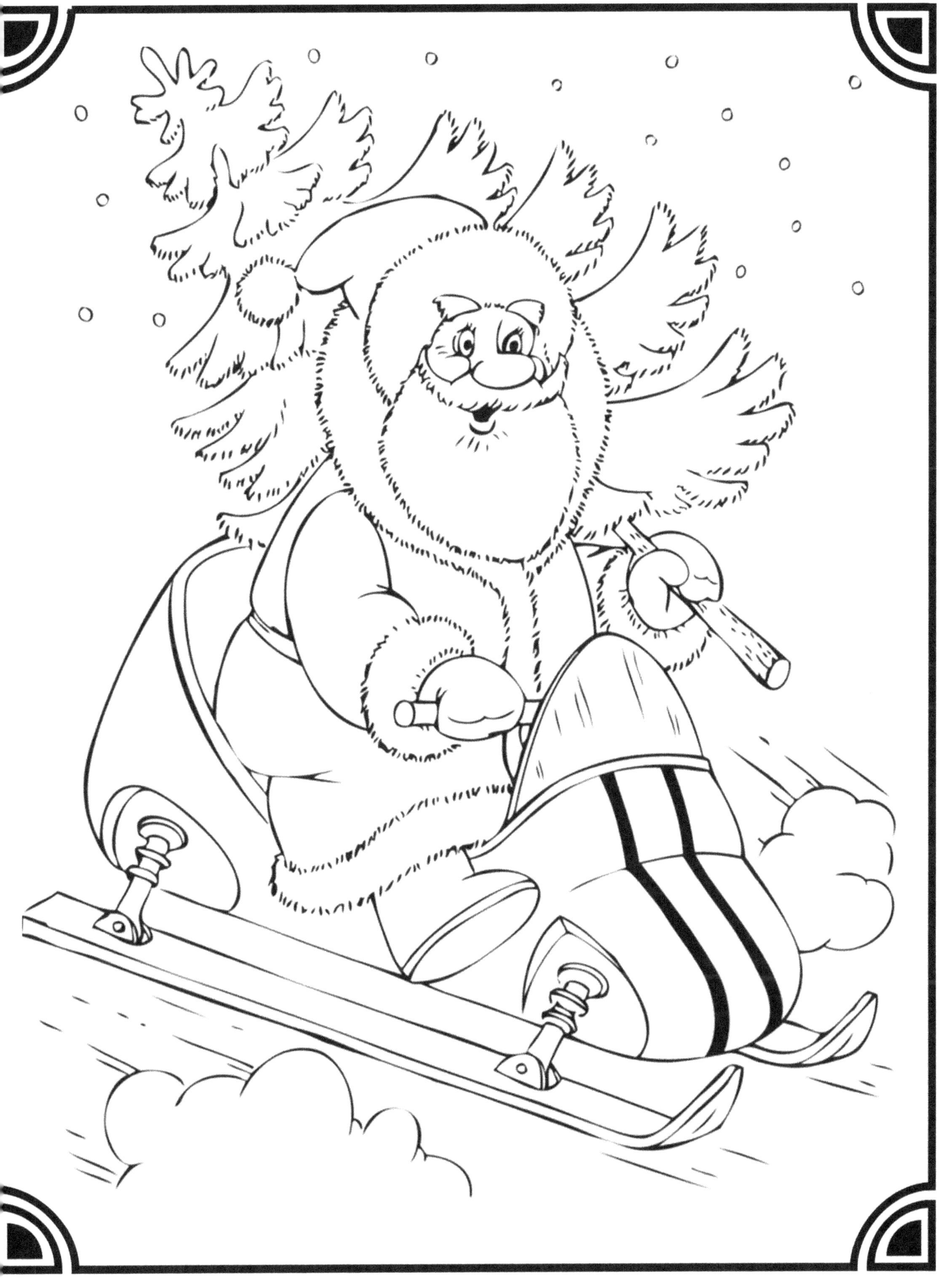

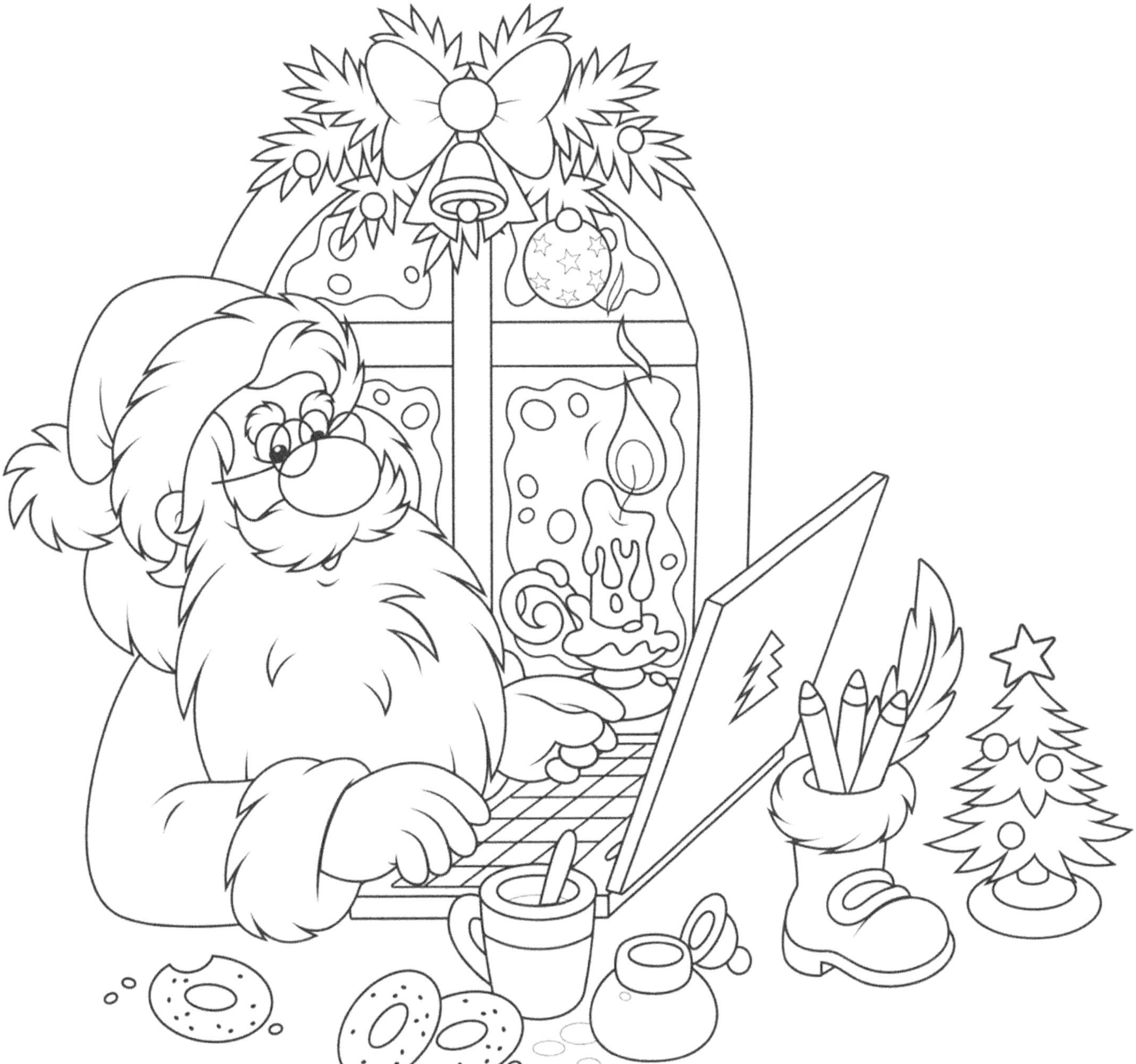

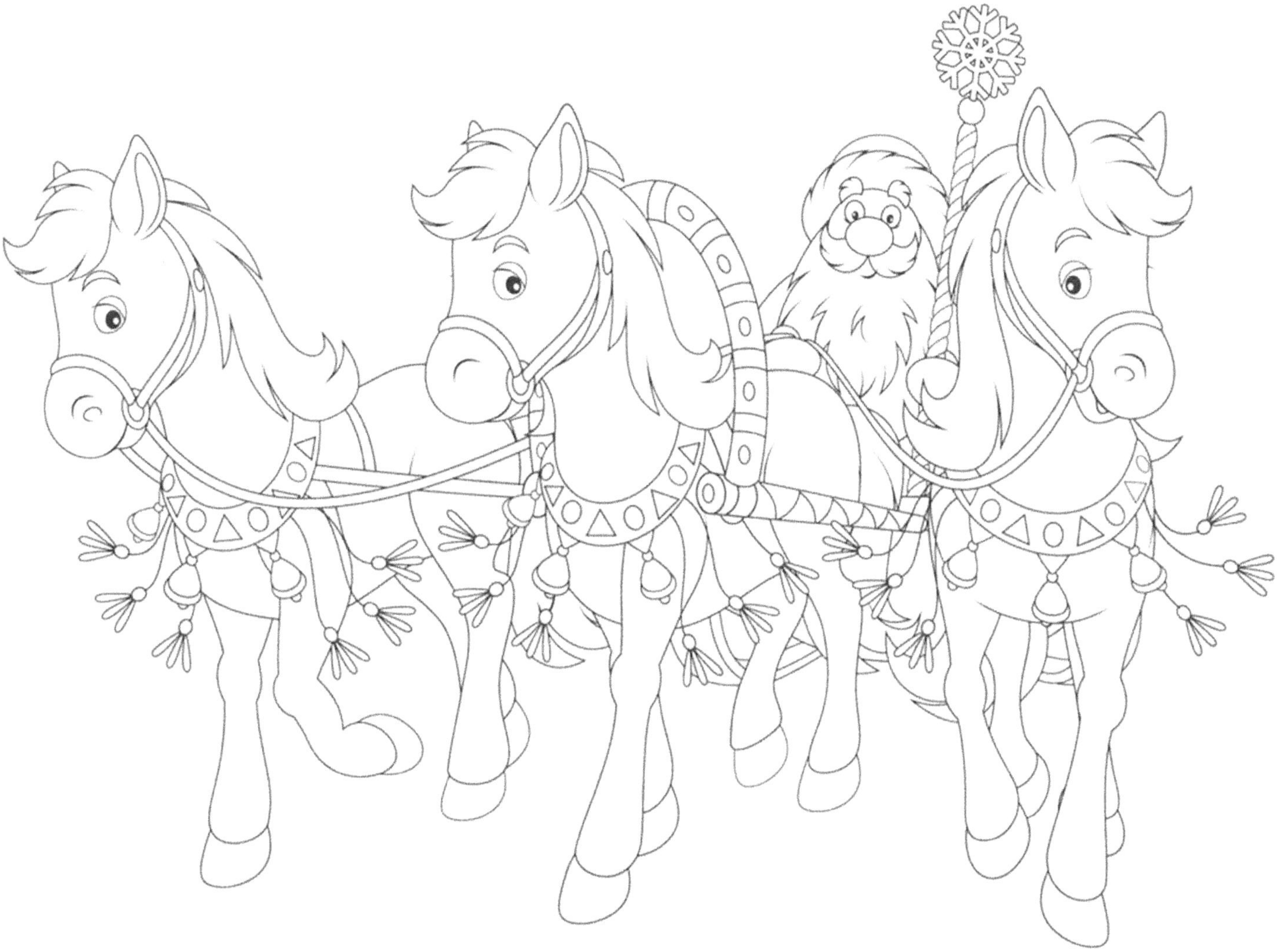

www.ingramcontent.com/pod-product-compliance
Lightning Source LLC
Chambersburg PA
CBHW081535220526
45467CB00010B/3195
*9781711687247*